"In this prophetically pugilistic book, Jonathan Walton has put into words so much of what troubles me about American Christianity. Like the best and most dangerous of interlocutors, Walton says things I'm not sure I agree with, breaks taboos I've been reluctant to break, and makes me think deeply enough to get uncomfortable. I recommend the discomfort of this book to every American seeking to take Jesus seriously today."

Gregory Coles, author of *Single, Gay, Christian*

"In a society in which Christianity and American culture have become intertwined in deeply unbiblical ways, this book is a breath of fresh air. It not only offers a challenging cultural critique but it also offers a constructive vision for how the kingdom of God might look in the American context. I strongly recommend this insightful and timely book."

Nathan Walton, executive director of Charlottesville Abundant Life Ministries

"I grew up in a Chinese American church that espoused biblical inerrancy, but still I was indoctrinated by white American folk religion and its syncretistic beliefs. Jonathan Walton, like a prophet in the wilderness, speaks God's truth to power and unmasks the idolatrous ways of American Christianity. May we listen, repent, and follow anew Jesus' radical call to pick up our crosses and follow him."

Russell Jeung, chair and professor of Asian American studies at San Francisco State University, author of *At Home in Exile*

"There's no denying that God is upsetting the American expression of Christianity in our time. Jonathan is masterful at jarring us and leading us all the same. It seems that the greatest obstacle to our nation experiencing the kind of peace we've longed for is continuing to believe that everything is okay. We need to cry—deeply and sincerely in order to begin to find the healing and freedom this nation needs. We need sharp and prophetic voices that are prepared to smash us to pieces for our own good. We need to be brought out of the deception of our own darkness and into the marvelous light of God's truth. I'd encourage anyone serious about their spiritual journey to take heed to Jonathan's words."

Rich Perez, pastor of teaching and vision at Christ Crucified Fellowship in New York City, author of *Mi Casa Uptown*

"Wounds don't heal if they are infected. In *Twelve Lies That Hold America Captive*, Jonathan Walton uncovers the idolatrous assumptions and infected lies that get in the way of America and Americans pursuing real change, healing, and shalom. Whatever your ethnic background, this smart, honest, and challenging work will make you examine your own heart and help you sort out the difference between the life-giving gospel of Scripture and the presuppositions of the American dream. If knowing the truth can set us free, there's freedom from idolatry and blindness that's offered in these pages."

Sarah Shin, author of *Beyond Colorblind*

"One part history, one part wake-up call, and all parts pastoral, Walton takes us on a transformative journey. Walton applies God's scriptural truth to the artifacts, sayings, and concepts that have formed the American imagination. With helpful historical context, he shows us how we got to where we are— and reveals the lies that we accidentally believe. With a unique combination of prophetic and pastoral, Walton gives practical and helpful tools to extract these lies and replace them with Jesus' truths and promises."

Nikki Toyama-Szeto, executive director of ESA/The Sider Center, coeditor of *God of Justice*

"Jonathan has a way with words. Better yet, he has a way with truth— understanding God's multifaceted truth and the truth of our history as a nation. Backed with these truths, a wide swath of compelling experiences, and a thorough belief in grace, *Twelve Lies That Hold America Captive* builds a compelling case about our dangerous idolatry that cannot be ignored. Whether you lean politically left or right, be prepared to be called out and brought to the transformative call of Jesus."

Yucan Chiu, director of The Ethnos Network, pastor of Ethnos New Brunswick Staff, graduate and faculty ministries at Rutgers University

"Jonathan Walton has a great gift of speaking the truth in love. In an age when striking this balance is rarely held, he offers us a way forward that doesn't dismiss difficult truths about the United States of America, nor does he simply diagnose the problem without offering us a way forward. To bear witness to Jesus and his kingdom requires us to live in truth without senti-mentalizing love. We cannot witness to the kingdom of God and be held captive to lies. Jonathan offers a compelling vision of what we can become, but only if we choose to see and reject the lies we've held."

Rich Villodas, lead pastor of New Life Fellowship, New York City

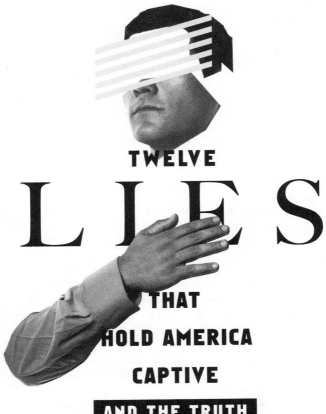

TWELVE
LIES

THAT
HOLD AMERICA
CAPTIVE

AND THE TRUTH
THAT SETS US FREE

JONATHAN P. WALTON

IVP Books

An imprint of InterVarsity Press
Downers Grove, Illinois

InterVarsity Press
P.O. Box 1400, Downers Grove, IL 60515-1426
ivpress.com
email@ivpress.com

InterVarsity Press® is the book-publishing division of InterVarsity Christian Fellowship/USA®, a movement of students and faculty active on campus at hundreds of universities, colleges, and schools of nursing in the United States of America, and a member movement of the International Fellowship of Evangelical Students. For information about local and regional activities, visit intervarsity.org.

Cover design: David Fassett
Interior design: Jeanna Wiggins
Image: © drbimages / iStock / Getty Images Plus

ISBN 978-0-8308-4558-3 (print)
ISBN 978-0-8308-7336-4 (digital)

Printed in the United States of America ♾

InterVarsity Press is committed to ecological stewardship and to the conservation of natural resources in all our operations. This book was printed using sustainably sourced paper.

Library of Congress Cataloging-in-Publication Data
A catalog record for this book is available from the Library of Congress.

P	23	22	21	20	19	18	17	16	15	14	13	12	11	10	9	8	7	6	5	4	3	2
Y	38	37	36	35	34	33	32	31	30	29	28	27	26	25	24	23	22	21	20	19		

For

God, our Father

Pauline Allen, my Momma

Priscilla, my wife

Maia, my daughter

**Thank you for
loving me for who I am,
not what I do for you.**

OPENING PRAYER

*May God bless you with discomfort at easy
answers, half-truths, and superficial relationships
so that you may live deep within your heart.*

*May God bless you with anger at injustice, oppression,
and exploitation of people and the planet that you
might work for justice, freedom, and peace.*

*May God bless you with tears to shed for those who suffer
pain, rejection, hunger, and war that you might reach out
your hand to comfort them and turn their pain to joy.*

*And may God bless you with enough foolishness to
believe that you can make a difference in the world, that
you can do what others claim cannot be done. To bring
justice, kindness, and the gospel to every corner of
creation, especially among all children and the poor.*

Amen.

A FRANCISCAN BLESSING, MODIFIED

CONTENTS

FOREWORD

Greg Jao

I WISH I COULD CLAIM that I was not an expert liar. Of course, that would be a lie. I suspect we all are expert liars. We lie a lot. We begin lying as children. I remember my toddlers insisting that they did not take the candy from the jar, even though they were standing in a pile of crumpled candy wrappers. As children, our lies are simple and easily detected. When we enter our teens, our lies become more complex, and our alibis become more convincing. It takes an observant (or lucky) parent to catch us. By the time we become adults, we have become experts at telling lies. We tell them so smoothly that they often pass undetected. We construct stories, situations, and systems to support them. We tell new lies to reinforce old lies. We sever or sabotage relationships to defend them. Our lies can be so well entrenched after twenty or thirty years that it requires an enormous crisis to confront them. Bankruptcy. Rehab. The loss of a job. The end of a marriage.

If this is true for us as individuals, imagine how hard it is to confront the lies of a nearly 250-year-old nation. What crisis would be big enough, visible enough, destructive enough to shatter our defenses and force us to face the truth? I hope it is the *crises* we are currently living in—the crises that Jonathan describes so carefully and passionately in this book. The stories and statistics Jonathan has assembled challenge our self-deception. They invite us to honest reflection as individuals and communities. They point us to a better way forward, one defined by Scripture rather than by the Stars and Stripes. But I worry because there can be tremendous resistance to letting go of the lies. We are invested in them.

Why do we lie as individuals, institutions, and nations? As an experienced liar, I know I tell lies because I want people to believe I am more courageous, more diligent, more loving, more careful, more competent, more faithful, and more holy than I really am. I tell lies so that I do not have to admit to myself—or others—that I am scared, insecure, selfish, sloppy, and sinful. I do not want to confront the truth that I fail (frequently) and am a failure (comprehensively). I am reluctant to face myself honestly. And my reluctance should be shocking because I am a Christian.

Christians should be the quickest to admit we fail (and are failures). The words "We have sinned. Will you forgive us?" should come easily to our lips. After all, these are the words that we said when we became Christians. They are the words that we say regularly to the triune God—and should be saying regularly to each other. These are the words that should cause no surprise or shock at a church. (What hospital would be shocked if a patient said, "I am sick"? Of course they are! That is why they are here.) And yet, tragically, these are words that we are reluctant to say. About ourselves. About our institutions. And about our country. As a result, we reject the truth. We quench the Spirit. We cheat ourselves out of the hope of restoration, renewal, and renovation. We deny the power of the gospel.

But what if this were not so?

Over the past decade, I have watched Jonathan help thousands of college students confront lies. Lies about themselves. (*I'm unforgiveable. Unredeemable. Unlovable.*) Lies about Scripture. (*It's oppressive. Irrelevant. Untrue.*) Lies about God. (*He's distant. Disinterested. Dangerous.*) And lies about our country that he uncovers in the chapters that follow. What I love and respect about Jonathan is that he is not content to name the lies. Any journalist or pundit could do that. Any self-appointed "prophet" does that. Jonathan does more. He points past the lies to Jesus—he who is the Truth and the source of truths that can set us all free.

As an expert liar, I long to be free of the lies that bind me and define me. I want to face reality in my life, in my church, and in my country. I want to embrace the truth so that God's truth can set me free. If you want the same, read this book. Rage over the stories. Grieve over the statistics. Wrestle with the ideas. Embrace the crisis it creates. Reject the lies. And seek the transforming truths that Jesus brings.

INTRODUCTION

THE LIES THAT BIND

In 2008, I felt like an American for the first time because I saw a leader who looked like me. All my life I hoped my education and accomplishments would free me from the history of my skin color as inherently inferior and forever intimidating. It never did. But then Barack Hussein Obama became president of the United States, and I believed that I belonged here.[1]

I watched his inauguration, and with each phrase I felt more optimistic. I thought, *Now things are going to be different*. One word defined Obama's campaign and resonated in communities around the country.

Hope.

It was on posters, buttons, and bumper stickers in all fifty states. Somehow, saying it over and over made it feel more possible. Hope seemed not like the perfect campaign strategy but something genuine and necessary. It sounded a lot better than mounting body counts in US prisons and soldiers not returning from Afghanistan and Iraq. Especially to me—a black male graduate of Columbia University who was unsure of my own ethnic identity, my place in this country, and my place in American Christianity.

I ask you to resist judgment, the urge to look away, and the opportunity to move on. I invite you to carry your skepticism through this entire book while leaning in to understand. Hold your gaze on the picture I am painting and consider its implications for how you think, speak, pray, and act. Your salvation is at stake, and your evangelism is compromised if you claim to be a follower of Jesus while building dividing walls of hostility and allowing them to govern your life. We are to be his witnesses, living differently in this world so we point others to him, and we cannot do that if we are not willing to engage with our differences to seek his justice and reflect his kingdom. I once lived this way, but because of Christ and for the sake of his gospel, I do so no longer.

Abraham Lincoln, Ronald Reagan, and Barack Obama claimed that the United States of America is the last and best hope for the world. As a follower of the Jesus of Scripture, this should have immediately drawn resistance from me. But it didn't because being a part of something bigger felt good. I can't see God, but I can see opportunity and seize it. To believe that I, a poor, black, and racially profiled man, could be a part of the hope for kids in Yemen, Somalia, and Honduras felt empowering. I felt important, included, and useful. I thought my life could matter. I believed my black life did matter. A shift was happening internally as I perceived things to be changing around me. Perhaps now, with a black president of the United States, I could be taken seriously, given the benefit of the doubt, and assumptions of fear and intimidation and anger toward me would lessen. I started to function as though the following were true about me too:

"We are the people we've been waiting for."

"Be the change you want to see in the world."

These quotes from Obama and Mahatma Gandhi, respectively, started to take over barbershop walls, T-shirts, and store windows.

It felt good to feel integral to the movement to make this country a better place. Not only could I belong to this country, but I also could contribute to and even lead its transformation. That is not the narrative I grew up hearing. It's the narrative I heard of white people, both here and abroad. The only place I felt valuable was in black churches. Gospel music and black preaching weren't theater, performance, or entertainment, but just us being us before the Lord. And now we, the ball dunkers, fast runners, and entertainers could also be legitimate leaders and key contributors to the future of this country, not just its slave labor. But then the American = white = male = Christian forcefully reasserted itself.

PRESS IN, DON'T LOOK AWAY

I urge you to acknowledge the tension you might feel but not judge or disengage. With your skepticism and questions fully present, would you hold them and continue onward with a heart tuned to understand? There is a deep need for peacemakers in this world, and we can only mend to the extent that we are willing to engage with what's broken.

The deaths at the hands of law enforcement of Trayvon Martin, Michael Brown, Eric Garner, Sandra Bland, Walter Scott, and the ever-growing list of African Americans now memorialized eroded any hope that formed in me. This realization continued for me as I came to understand that this was a problem not only for my immediate ethnic community but also for those I had previously been unable to consider because of the blindness induced by the plight of my own people. Native peoples in America make up the highest percentage of police-involved killings, and the Latinx community suffers numbers comparable to the black community. Both experience the plight of invisibility with little to no media coverage.[2]

The weight of this compelled me to pray, write, march, and organize. These were all efforts to feel seen, heard, validated, and valued in a culture that casts me and other people of color as dangerous and disposable.

More poignantly, I remember sitting in a Sunday service on the Upper East Side of New York City the day after George Zimmerman was acquitted. The worship leader opened with a time of prayer and invited the congregation to pray aloud. Prayers for sick family members, a husband looking for a job, friends in need of healing, and more people to know Jesus filled the air. I was waiting. Waiting for anybody except me—the only black person in the room—to say "God bless the family of Trayvon Martin." No one did. The "church" that was supposed to be my sanctuary did not see Trayvon, so this church didn't see me; if it did see Trayvon, his black life wasn't worth mentioning. His black life didn't matter, and if I met the same unjust demise, my black life wouldn't matter either. The pastor would stand before a congregation segregated by race and class with the proclaimed desire to be inclusive, but when prayers are invited, no prayers would be offered for marginalized communities that were not in the room.

When Terence Crutcher was killed in Tulsa, Oklahoma, I had never felt so disposable. Grief was unlocked within me, and I wept in bed beside my wife, Priscilla, trying to make sense of a country that did not want me. America's systemic oppression of the poor and people of color were illuminated again by police murder. This, coupled with unparalleled protection and empowerment of those with privilege and power, left me depressed and in a daze.

I had to confess this is the country and the American church I'm a part of. The church that I long to belong to doesn't avoid injustice, silence dissidents, and ignore oppression. It doesn't tell me to *know my place and stay in it* with a station lower than my lighter-skinned neighbors. The family of Christ is a beloved community, but what I so often experienced was fear triumphing over love on a daily basis inside and outside the church, in person and online.

In 2015, the *Guardian* reported that 1,134 people were killed by police in the United States.[3] And that number is only an estimate because it is still not mandatory to report these deaths to the Justice Department, FBI, or any other government agency.[4] And despite being 5 percent of the population of the United States, African American males make up 15 percent of these deaths.[5] These statistics only added to my feelings of disposability. Men and women who look like me, my momma, and my small group Bible study could end up as hashtags simply for "fitting the description."

The lack of compassion and acknowledgment of systemic pain and suffering when a killing is broadcast online and in the news is deeply hurtful. The pain intensifies as the silence of indifference reverberates through vulnerable communities along with the vocal, visible, inaccurate, and retaliatory actions and dialogues that ensue after a broadcast of police brutality. But most excruciating is the disregard for the pain and suffering that those with "the privilege of moving on" exhibit on a regular basis in the church. I should not have to convince a pastor that police brutality is a gospel issue. My fear should not be dismissed or need substantiation. The conscious and unconscious fear of people of color needs to be dealt with, not swept away. Yet with every meeting, email, and Facebook debate with my supposed brothers and sisters in Christ, I felt less and less like family and more like a stray dog who was allowed to be around but to never belong. I was in someone else's Father's house.

Prayer requests, sermons, podcasts, seminars, discipleship tools, and other components of American Christianity enmeshed with white American culture remain largely unchanged amid political polarization and rising inequality. In 2016, some of America's most famous "Christian" leaders and institutions doubled down on bigotry, homophobia, racism, and Islamophobia. These leaders reinforced their defense of gun lobbyists, silence on sexual assault, and endorsement of greed and militarism throughout the election cycle. This reality isn't just ideological but has real-life implications, as 81 percent of white evangelicals voted for Donald Trump while 88 percent of African Americans voted against him.[6] To claim that the white American church does not embody and enforce the ethnic, social, and political division and call it "Christian" is to live in denial. And to stop reading here because you disagree is cowardice.

GRAPPLING WITH THE REALITIES OF HISTORY

Followers of Jesus must wrestle with what it means to have an authoritative, distinctly Christian witness in our context—not one rooted in American political power, clout, and relevance driven by talk radio, Christian conferences, and televangelism. All people must be called out of what I call White American Folk Religion (WAFR).[7]

Historically, the US Constitution protects a self-determined superior race of people called "whites." White supremacy was and is sin—intentional and unconfessed. WAFR takes that premise and goes further. It ensures that men will hold power over women by giving men control of wealth, the right to vote, and the ability and preference to hold political office. Laws, amendments, and ordinances enshrine the institution of slavery, unjust distribution of wealth, and the segregation and subjugation of ethnic groups, women, and the poor. This includes Jewish immigrants and those from Europe, Asia, Latin America, and Africa. The court system has the power to take the lives of poor people who have committed crimes, the unborn, mentally ill, or those deemed feeble-minded.

Alongside these implications are the profound differences between the teachings and practices of Jesus in Scripture and those of WAFR. The United States and the kingdom of God are antithetical to one another. I once wondered how we got here. Now I know—this is where we have always been. We see this in the following laws and social norms:

- *1790*. Before this year, the United States did not have a national policy for voting. This law stated that "free White men of good standing" could vote. Prior to that, only white men over the age of twenty-one and who owned property (including owning women and slaves) were eligible to vote in most states. Therefore, Native Americans, slaves, free blacks, women, indentured servants, the poor, and immigrants from Asia and Latin America were not citizens and therefore barred from the political process.[8]

- *1857*. Dred Scott, a free black slave, saw his freedom taken away via a Supreme Court decision that set the stage for the Civil War.

- *1858–1865*. Abraham Lincoln is held in high regard for penning the Emancipation Proclamation, but he did not believe that all people were made in the image of God. In the fourth presidential debate at Charleston, Illinois, on September 18, 1858, Lincoln cleared up any controversy when he was accused of promoting "negro equality": "I will say then that I am not, nor ever have been, in favor of bringing about in any way the social and political equality of the white and black races." Lincoln also "opposed blacks having the right to vote, to serve on juries, to hold office and to intermarry with whites. What he did believe was that, like all men, blacks had the right to improve their condition in society and to enjoy the fruits of their labor. In this way they were equal to white men, and for this reason slavery was inherently unjust." [9] Lincoln did not believe that blacks and whites should or could live peaceably and favored colonization as the solution to this insurmountable problem. This colonization would have been mass deportation of people of color to South America and the Caribbean.

- *1882.* The Chinese Exclusion Act signed by President Chester Arthur halted all immigration from China until 1943. This permanently separated thousands of men from their wives and children.

- *1887.* The Dawes Act made it possible for Native Americans to vote if they gave up their tribal affiliation and dissolved their governments and rights to land.

- *1893.* American diplomatic and military personnel conspired to illegally overthrow the monarchy of the Hawaiian kingdom. Queen Liliuokalani was stripped of power and land ownership, and voting rights were restricted for Hawaiians. Then in 1898, despite formal opposition, the United States imposed military occupation and unilaterally annexed the island to utilize its position for the Spanish American War. The Hawaiian kingdom's latest complaint, filed with the United Nations in 2001, continued to protest their illegal occupation by the United States.

- *1906.* The San Francisco Board of Education ordered the segregation of Asian children into separate public elementary schools. They justified segregation as a measure "to save white children from being affected by association with pupils of the Mongolian race."[10]

- *1922.* In *Takao Ozawa v. United States,* the US Supreme Court ruled that persons of Japanese origin are insufficiently white to qualify for citizenship.[11] This move bolstered movements such as the Asiatic Exclusion League and led to the Chinese Exclusion Act. It also planted seeds for Japanese internment during World War II and other prejudiced laws and social norms that persist to this day.

- *1923.* The US Supreme Court declared persons of Indian descent, even "high caste Hindus," as ineligible for citizenship because they could not be legally recognized as white persons.[12]

- *1927.* The Supreme Court Decision *Buck v. Bell* upheld the decision to allow forced sterilizations of those deemed "imbeciles." Justice Oliver Wendell Holmes infamously wrote in the decision, "three generations of imbeciles are enough." This meant that more than 70,000 impoverished, disabled, and mentally ill persons, as well as women deemed too interested in sex, were prevented from having children by the US government via forced sterilization.[13]

- *1929–1936.* The Mexican Repatriation during the Great Depression removed between 500,000 and 2 million people from the United States. They were accused of stealing jobs by the attorney general, and Ford Motor Company and Southern Pacific Railroad encouraged employees to go back to their own people.[14] At the same time, states began to cut welfare to these citizens.

- *1946–1958.* The United States infected hundreds of people in Guatemala with gonorrhea and syphilis without their knowledge in collaboration with the Guatemalan government, which America strongly influenced.[15] Ultimately, the CIA would overthrow the government to ensure land use for the multinational corporation United Fruit Company.[16]

- Felony conviction leads to loss of voting rights in many states to this day, which affects 2.5 percent of the US population. A high percentage of those people are from communities of color or areas with a high concentration of poverty.[17]

The infusion of government structures with a legal, deceptive "fear of the other" stands in opposition to the biblical mandate for us to love our neighbors (Mark 12:31) and care for the stranger in our midst as if they were native born (Leviticus 19:34).

Followers of Jesus believe that reconciliation through Christ is the only way to attain an eternal identity through adoption into an everlasting covenantal love, which is what all people of every background and ethnicity profoundly need. American history composed by white, wealthy men was written to argue otherwise. The Bible, however, exclaims that we do not need citizenship, voting rights, or access to property and capital, but a constant, unchanging status in Christ Jesus, which cannot be taken away. All of humanity is in need of a home, but that home is not the United States or any place. It is a person, and his name is Jesus.

RESIST THE IDOLATRY OF AMERICA

So this is where we begin our journey. In each chapter, I will discuss a dominant lie in our culture, how it is in opposition to the gospel, and how living within these false narratives compromises our Christian witness and leads to division and destruction. Moreover, I will provide stories of what it looks like to pursue an ever-deepening union with God in love, in direct resistance to the idols that seek to remove Christ from our hearts. Last, I will describe accounts of lives lived in freedom among people who have yet to experience the freedom of Jesus, exemplifying how we might bear witness to him like the early Christians in Acts 1–7 along with next steps for you to take.

I believed these twelve lies because I believed falsely that in the face of oppression and adversity I could hold myself together with grit, hard work, and resilience. I see these destructive patterns at work on campuses and around kitchen tables in every region of the United States whether it's among people born here or now living here but from elsewhere. These lies are at work among donors with millions of dollars and with those who have no homes. As the director of InterVarsity's New York City Urban Project, I often found myself at intersections of race, class, status, and sexual orientation, where the invitation to worship something other than Jesus was always present. Instead of abiding in Christ (John 15) and finding abundance, growth, discipline, and identity in Jesus, I chose to follow the American dream. And so many of us are doing the same.

The dream so profoundly called for by Martin Luther King Jr. was not the American dream but a longing for the kingdom of God. Clouded by my longing for inclusion and significance, I believed the lies and bought into the gospel of America. All I had to do was accept my invitation to pursue life, liberty, and happiness. In the words of Denzel Washington, playing Malcolm X in the movie of the same name, I was "hoodwinked, bamboozled. Led astray."[18] I was willing, like so many other Christians, to receive America in exchange for the kingdom of God.

Many Christians hold the same level of commitment to the Pledge of Allegiance that they hold to the Apostles' Creed. I thought I was following Jesus when I was actually a cultural Christian and a biblical hypocrite. Jesus is inviting us, just as he did the first disciples in Luke 5, to put down our nets (the twelve lies) and pursue a life with him. And that invitation is as pertinent today as it was two thousand years ago. He invites us to trust him and push out into deep water. He beckons us to witness his power because of faith and obedience. And finally, he invites us to stop our false pursuits, deny ourselves, take up our cross, and follow him.

As an experiential discipleship director, it is my privilege to lead one-day, week-long, and two-month leadership development programs. God called me to stand on the bridge between the rich and poor—physically and spiritually—and journey with those desiring to walk with Christ in this way. We require anyone in our programs to journey with at least one other person, so I hope you are turning these pages with a neighbor who is different from you in some way. We also ask anyone participating in our programs to begin each day by praying corporately. As we journey together, please pray this Franciscan prayer with me.

God bless us with discomfort at easy answers,
half-truths and superficial relationships,
so that we may live deep within our hearts.

God bless us with righteous anger at injustice, oppression,
and exploitation of people and the planet,
so that we might work for justice, freedom, and peace.

God bless us with tears to shed for those who suffer pain,
rejection, hunger, and war,
so that we might turn their pain into joy.

And God bless us with enough foolishness
to believe that we can make a difference in the world,
so that we might do what others claim cannot be done.
To bring justice, kindness and the gospel to all people,
especially the poor.

STOP AND REFLECT

- What were your dominant feelings as you read this introduction: curiosity, surprise, confusion, numbness, familiarity, distance, or something else?
- What phrases, stories, or historical events resonated with you?
- What events or narratives were you unaware of? What did you learn?
- Where do you disagree, or have concerns, or want to stop reading?
- What questions are you carrying into the next chapter?

LIE 1

WE ARE A CHRISTIAN NATION

"LIFE, LIBERTY AND THE PURSUIT OF HAPPINESS," as defined by the founders of America, are different from the promises of the living God. In fact, white American folk religion places life in America as preferred, even superior to the abundant life offered by Jesus.

I know this now, but I didn't know it in 2004. I arrived at Columbia University in the fall of 2004 from Brodnax, a small town in south-central Virginia. It lacked a stoplight, bank, and we had no supermarket —but there were a lot of churches. When I arrived at college, I was asked by friends if I was "Reformed" and had no idea what those in the "Christian Fellowship" were talking about. John Piper, Tim Keller, Mark Driscoll, TobyMac, and Dispatch had nothing to do with my Christianity. The Gospel Coalition, *Christianity Today*, and C. S. Lewis were not on my reading list. I had never been on a mission trip, visited a Young Life camp, or attended a church that used PowerPoint. I knew the Soul Stirrers and John P. Kee, and sang from hymnals to beats made by clapping hands and patting feet. InterVarsity, Redeemer Presbyterian Church, and many *Christian* spaces I sat in showed me a different Jesus from the one I grew up with. Over time, I started to believe that the Jesus introduced to me at Meherrin Baptist Church in Brodnax was less than ideal at best and heretical at worst. The pastors who baptized and discipled me changed in my mind from committed men of God to *liberation theologians*, *prosperity preachers*, and *motivational speakers* who were light on doctrine. The women who taught from the pulpit went from prophetic leaders to disobedient females.[1]

Of course, not everything I was taught in Sunday school was biblical, but I had never felt less than another believer, and that's what I felt sitting in InterVarsity's weekly worship service at Columbia. Black preachers were rare, the songs familiar to me were never sung, and inductive Bible study was a prized method for engaging Scripture. I came to believe that it wasn't that I worshiped *differently*, but that I worshiped *incorrectly*. The songs they sang were how we are *supposed* to sing. The way they prayed was how Christians are *supposed* to pray. "They," in this story, are my white American brothers and sisters, and the mostly international Chinese students that stood beside them. Being in a majority-white American and Chinese crowd, I felt alone, isolated, and demoralized, but I did my best to assimilate. There was one other non-Asian-specific campus ministry, so with only two choices, I went all-in. I behaved similarly in my classes but experienced a similar separateness. In a theater class there was an option to learn and perform "black preaching." Not only was the teaching I sat under as a child unbiblical, but also in this new culture it was entertainment.

Through my years at Columbia, issues of race and ethnicity boiled underneath the surface of our campus Christian fellowship. But at a retreat during my junior year, our campus minister invited a speaker to share God's vision for multiethnicity and invited us to lament, confess, repent, and practice genuine reconciliation with Christ at the center.

During a response time to the teaching that was presented, my best friend and I were made to sit on opposite sides of the room. We were reminded that in America we have racial assignments. In the United States I am black and he is white. Instead of being two people made in the image of God, navigating difference as best we can, we were thrust back into our boxes. This black-and-white divide was highlighted on campus but never this blatant. We were given the biblical mandate and social invitation to engage, which was the beginning of long nights and dialogues between us that continue to this day.

I'm grateful for the speaker's leadership, specifically her ability to guide all ethnic backgrounds through this tension and not over or around it. While I was having this hard but liberating experience, one of my white brothers was profoundly uncomfortable and openly asked for it to stop. I felt heartbroken and afraid of being pushed back to the margins. Thankfully, some continued to press in. I carry sadness to this day about the dissonance that experience caused in my heart and in the lives of those around me. There was a clear break between us, and we reflected the chasm between the two groups in our fellowship. There were those who embraced the privilege of moving on and those whose skin color and personal experience didn't afford them the same opportunity. Jesus came to break down the dividing walls of hostility, and he commissioned us to walk in that ministry. Some decided not to follow him that day. That disengagement is a part of WAFR.

Lament, confession, repentance, and reconciliation are clearly parts of Jesus' gospel and the disciples' lives, but they are not part of American Christian culture. What many practice and promote in America passes for genuine faith in Christ, but 80 percent of Christians don't read the Bible daily. Furthermore, only 1 percent of Christians in America believe we are doing discipleship well, as reported by the Barna Group.[2]

When we don't meet Christ in Scripture and are not regularly being discipled by or discipling others, it is impossible to discern what being a Christian means or to cultivate a relationship with God. This lack of intimacy with Jesus and his people doesn't take into account those who claim to be Christians but see justice, reconciliation, and compassion as optional Christian activities. Nor does it capture the number of those who believe in Jesus' divinity or status as a "great teacher" but not exclusively as the way, the truth, and the life (John 14:6). Scripture, however, makes it clear that all of these are essential to the faith.

The first lie that holds America captive is that the United States is a Christian nation. This is false for many reasons. Chief among them is that people who practice WAFR live incompatibly with biblical Christianity because WAFR is not rooted in a relationship with Jesus, compromises genuine witness to Jesus, and is void of faith in Christ. Moreover, WAFR requires the exchange of the kingdom of God for the United States of America. Jesus didn't come to earth to establish any nation as Christian—including the United States (Acts 1).

WHAT IS WHITE AMERICAN FOLK RELIGION (WAFR)?

By *white* I mean the system created to claim that those of darker skin color are inherently inferior. Over time, *white* included components of family, national background, or class. At its core, whiteness was created solely to subjugate one group of people and elevate the other. In Europe and the Americas, it is the subjugation of indigenous people, those descended from Africa, Asia, and Latin America, as well as women, the materially poor, and social outcasts. *America* is the context where this ideology reigns most strongly. And *folk religion* is the common set of popular beliefs and practices under the guise of true religion but outside of the faith's official doctrines and practices. WAFR claims to be biblical Christianity.

In WAFR, early American leaders such as George Washington and Thomas Jefferson are moved from mere leaders to forefathers, as if to make all Americans their descendants. Instead of being made in the image of God, we live in the shadow of the images on Mount Rushmore. The men are transformed into mythical figures. Our freedom then was not afforded by the blood of Jesus but by the blood of soldiers who took and defended our right to liberty. Our Father is not Yahweh but a nonspecific Creator, and the Bible is replaced by the Constitution. Instead of the Ten Commandments, we have the first ten Amendments, known as the Bill of Rights. The law and our leaders, not the Messiah, will set us free because we trust in our representatives and equate the president with our Savior. This narrative isn't just false, it's idolatrous; we center our identities on the accomplishments of men, not God and his will for all creation.

HOW TO PRACTICE WHITE AMERICAN FOLK RELIGION

WAFR not only deifies its leaders, but like every false ideology, it has a method of worship, praise, and sacrifice that reveal its followers' membership and level of dedication. WAFR has three key practices:

1. the regular tithe of time, money, and talent to pursue personal comfort and selfish ambition

2. covert and overt efforts to uphold a race-, gender-, and class-based hierarchy

3. corporate orientation and accountability around pleasure-seeking and consumption

These three tenets are implied in the Declaration of Independence: "We hold these truths to be self-evident, that all men are created equal, that they are endowed by their Creator with certain unalienable Rights, that among these are Life, Liberty and the pursuit of Happiness."

"Life, Liberty and the pursuit of Happiness" are promised by America and by God. But they are not the same in origin, practice, or motive. The goals and intentions of the Declaration of Independence sit in opposition to the gospel of Christ. The totality of Scripture does not endorse the marriage of God and country or the establishment, development, or practices of any country in the name of Jesus. The United States cannot be a Christian nation, because God's plan for redemption does not include a nation-state, and the beliefs and practices of WAFR are opposed to the arc of Scripture.

JESUS AND THE KU KLUX KLAN

Romans 12:1 states, "Do not be conformed to the pattern of this world, but be transformed by the renewing of your mind" (NIV). And in Romans 13 we see that Jesus' followers are to remain subject to civil laws and ordinances, respecting leaders and officers. There is an inherent tension between the kingdom of God and the disorder of the world.

The early church exemplifies what it looks like to bear witness within this tension. In Acts 6, when Greek widows were overlooked in the daily distribution of food because of their ethnic/cultural identity (not Hebrew), class (widow, poor), and gender (female), the disciples went against the patterns of the day and did not judge them by the world's standards. The apostles appointed seven Greek men full of the Spirit and wisdom to take over the daily food distribution. Culturally, these powerful male leaders had every right to overlook and even cast out these widowed and impoverished Greek women, who had few, if any, rights. But according to the way of Christ, there is no basis to favor the wealthy and connected (James 2:1-13). Scripture mandates that Christians prioritize the poor and remain always in their company in loving service (Matthew 25:31-46; 26:11).

Moreover, 2 Corinthians 5:16-21 is a crucial part of the apostle Paul's letter to the church at Corinth. This letter, like other narratives of the Acts church, sets up a system in opposition to the way their present world works. Paul says that followers of Christ are no longer to make assumptions and judgments based on the outward appearances of people and the standards of this world. Therefore, the founders of this country should not have sanctioned, promoted, and practiced slavery. They should not have ordained, participated in, or defended genocide and land theft. But that is precisely what happened. This heresy was not just practiced by authors of the Constitution but also by white pastors and leaders who filled the ranks of the Ku Klux Klan:

The goal of the *United Northern and Southern Knights of the Ku Klux Klan* is to unite White Christians through the bond of brotherhood and aid their awareness of the problems facing our country. We will show you how and when to take action (in a non violent way). The United Northern and Southern Knights of the Ku Klux Klan is a patriotic, fraternal and law abiding organization. We uphold Christian values this country was founded on. We protect these values from those who seek to remove them from our society. Our ideology is simple, self preservation and the advancement of White Christian America.[3]

Genesis 1:26-27 boldly states that every person is made in the image of God. And the two creation accounts in Genesis 1–2 expound on humanity's mandate to flourish, work, rule, and create. Yet leaders of the United States, instead of being rooted in the patterns of God, instituted a pattern of life oriented around the Protestant work ethic—the view that a person's duty is to achieve success through hard work and thrift, with such success being a sign that one has received salvation.[4] This system, which linked human worthiness to productivity alongside a race- and class-based social hierarchy, became the measure of a person's worth in our society. We internalize this value system and pass it on to those around us. And so it reigns to this day in the hearts of men and women, and in the institutions in which we operate and lead.

THE IDOLATRY OF WHITE AMERICAN FOLK RELIGION

The three key practices of WAFR mentioned earlier make it incompatible with biblical Christianity. These are not fringe practices or beliefs held only by a small group of people. George W. Bush famously invited Americans not to pray, give, or volunteer after the attacks on September 11, 2001, but to shop.[5] Barack Obama, on the day of his inauguration, January 20, 2009, stated that "we will not change our way of life, nor will we waver in its defense."[6] These are not invitations to radical generosity and selflessness, but affirmations that we will do things the way we have always done them. The idols of materialism, militarism, racism, and sexuality will not be destroyed by the passing of time or the hard work of a few because the race-based meritocracy at work in America is central to our way of life; held together by taking Scripture out of context and applying it with no regard for what Jesus actually preached, practiced, and called us to be.

The most infamous example of this proof texting or text-jacking is the Ku Klux Klan, whose charters and members proclaim that the burning cross is simultaneously a symbol of purification of the white race and Christ as the light of the world.[7] Many early Klansmen were Southern Baptist preachers marrying white supremacy with their misinterpreted Bible. Religious manipulation has been present since America's formation; so has selfish ambition for personal comfort. They undergird America's brand of capitalism and pleasure-at-any-cost mentality, requiring an endless stream of financial resources and allocation of time and talent toward those ends.

Victor Lebow, an influential twentieth-century economist, said,

> Our enormously productive economy demands that we make consumption our way of life, that we convert the buying and use of goods into rituals, that we seek our spiritual satisfactions, our ego satisfactions, in consumption. The measure of social status, of social acceptance, of prestige, is now to be found in our consumptive patterns. . . . We need things consumed, burned up, worn out, replaced and discarded at an ever increasing pace. [8]

In WAFR, wealth and power, not God's love, grace, and providence, give us identity, worth, and value. And American Catholics, Protestants, and evangelicals have absorbed, spread, and reinforced the values of WAFR and called them doctrine.

Greed, racialization, and comfort are opposed to Jesus' call to deny ourselves, take up our cross, and follow him. The unholy trinity of selfishness, racial animus, and pleasure-seeking is far from what the Father, Son, and Holy Spirit intend for humanity. But for this patently un-Christian pursuit of "life, liberty, and happiness" to continue, people must be held in a hierarchy where some are elevated and others subjugated, while the illusion of attainable equality and opportunity for progress is impeccably maintained. This social hierarchy is the structure that keeps one group protecting its power and resources while pushing the marginalized group to pursue the wealth and power it believes it must possess to belong.

Contrary to this worldview, the apostle Paul says, "If anyone is in Christ, *he is* a new creature; the old things passed away; behold, new things have come" (2 Corinthians 5:17). Followers of Jesus do not love others because of an amendment, a Supreme Court decision, or an executive order; we see others through the redemptive blood of Jesus. Followers of WAFR cannot claim to hold fast to biblical teaching. Segregation by race, gender, location, and social class reveals an allegiance to the words of the American forefathers, not to the word of God through Paul.

Through Jesus, God redefines the models for family and relationships. In Christ, there is no "other" and no basis for *us* versus *them*. Through Jesus Christ, our Father made a way for all humans—his image bearers—to be sons and daughters.

Paul says,

> You are all sons of God through faith in Christ Jesus. For all of you who were baptized into Christ have clothed yourselves with Christ. There is neither Jew nor Greek, there is neither slave nor free man, there is neither male nor female; for you are all one in Christ Jesus. And if you belong to Christ, then you are Abraham's descendants, heirs according to promise. (Galatians 3:26-29)

This is precisely where WAFR and its evangelists (e.g., Franklin Graham, Tony Perkins, Jerry Falwell Jr.) twist the Scriptures to pursue a false peace punctuated by the profound lack of lament, repentance, reconciliation, and justice. This false gospel, derived from popular, out-of-context interpretation, promotes unbiblical perspectives like colorblindness. *Colorblindness* is the well-intentioned, misinformed belief that by not acknowledging the present racial hierarchy we will finally be able to see one another as human and consequently live in harmony. Someone who values colorblindness might say "I don't see color" or "Racism is a sin problem, not a skin problem."

It would be profound and desirable if colorblindness automatically leveled the playing field, but it doesn't. In fact, saying "I don't see color" only makes matters worse. It strips all people, including those labeled "white," of their God-given ethnic identity and keeps all people from bringing their oppression and privilege to Jesus. Colorblindness is one way WAFR twists Scripture to force submission to the dominant culture, thus protecting white Jesus.

The Galatians and Corinthians passages are not endorsements of colorblindness or some amorphous goal that all people will arrive at when Jesus returns. They are a foretaste of the kingdom of heaven accessible now in Christ. These Scriptures, read alongside Revelation 7:9-10 and Revelation 21:1-8, give a glimpse of what the city of God is like.

Like a good symphony, Revelation 7:9-10 is layered with tension. There is a direct indictment against the reverse oppression that happens when an oppressed group wields power and chooses to subjugate those who violated them. In Revelation 7 we see *"all* tribes and peoples and tongues," which must include the once powerful *and* the once powerless. In the kingdom of God, there is no oppressed or oppressor, because the power structures as we know them do not exist. The love of Christ has torn them down. All people live under the loving reign and rule of Christ Jesus (2 Corinthians 5:18).

Followers of WAFR believe that the truths espoused in the Bill of Rights were divinely inspired and that the Declaration of Independence is what gives humanity a firm identity and inherent value. Ironically its authors did not value or extend the same rights to the poor, women, the indigenous, the enslaved, indentured servants, or certain immigrant groups. This system put in place by wealthy white males seeks to preserve their power. Their supposed powers include the ability to declare a person's humanness, to determine who is worthy of rights, and to grant identity, belonging, and agency. This is idolatry. Any person or group claiming the ability to declare human value or worth takes the place of God. True leadership, according to Christ, entails leveraging one's power and influence for the least of these, not for self-preservation or selfish gain.

Furthermore, to say America is a Christian nation admits a type of illiteracy and dismisses verifiable evidence that the purposes of God Almighty have been violated. To claim WAFR and biblical Christianity are the same replaces the need for confession and repentance with a list of ways to achieve *whiteness*. This false righteousness does not include being reconciled with God through Christ!

WAFR scrubs the power of Christ-centered activism out of messages from prophetic leaders such as Dr. Martin Luther King Jr. to construct a motivational glass half-full progressivism in place of a vision of the kingdom of God accomplished through Christ. For example, in a 1965 speech, King said,

> I believe it because somehow the arc of the moral universe is long but it bends toward justice. We shall overcome because Carlyle is right: "No lie can live forever." We shall overcome because William Cullen Bryant is right: "Truth crushed to earth will rise again." We shall overcome because James Russell Lowell is right: "Truth forever on the scaffold, wrong forever on the throne. Yet, that scaffold sways the future and behind the dim unknown standeth God within the shadow, keeping watch above his own." With this faith, we will be able to hew out of the mountain of despair a stone of hope. With this faith, we will be able to transform the jangling discords of our nation into a beautiful symphony of brotherhood. With this faith we will be able to speed up the day. [9]

Regularly this quote is whittled down to "the moral arc of the universe bends towards justice" by those who speak of a manmade redemption in which Jesus is just another "good teacher"; they promise to identify and end injustices on human terms.

Let me note that those who seek the common good *are* doing valuable work. However, this oft-used quote is an example of those in power choosing to cherry-pick sermons, speeches, and prayers to maintain our culture's present orientation around racism, materialism, militarism, and sexuality.

Conservative commentator Matt Lewis of the *Daily Beast* interviewed Michael Wear, who directed faith outreach for President

Obama's 2012 reelection. Wear says King's phrase has been used "to bless a whole range of political solutions." Lewis observes,

> The famous line, Wear notes, was originally intended as a spiritual truth, not a political one. "It's very clear that, apart from Jesus Christ, the idea of a moral arc of the universe was inconceivable to King," Wear told me during a recent interview. "It only made sense within the context of a declarative faith statement."[10]

Martin Luther King was shot because he preached and practiced allegiance to a different kingdom and rigorously opposed our present system. The Declaration of Independence, exploitative capitalism, and the Civil Rights Act are *not* the good news of the gospel of Jesus. The idea that they are is a false gospel because it is good news for neither those on the margins of society nor those enshrined with power by this nation's founding documents.

THE GOOD NEWS OF THE GOSPEL

Contrary to WAFR, the apostle Paul says that the love and grace of God and adoption into his family is not conditioned on our gender, skin color, or citizenship, but on a right relationship with God in Christ. Therefore, confession and repentance are essential, requiring reflection on our own brokenness and acceptance that humans are incapable of righting our individual and collective wrongs by ourselves. The gospel of Jesus Christ places total trust in God, who adopts us into his family, regardless of our background. The power of Christ is evident in 2 Corinthians 5:19-20, where Paul emphasizes the redemptive role of Jesus, the profound grace extended to us, and our inability to make things right with God and others on our own.

This personal, relational, and social impact is of great importance when contrasting WAFR with biblical Christianity, because America's assorted brands of Jesus proclaim something other than the crucified King, the family he calls us to, and the kingdom that is coming. In Acts 1:8, women and men who follow Jesus are commissioned to be witnesses filled with the Holy Spirit's power and sent to the ends of the earth. Per the Declaration of Independence, men are endowed with inalienable rights from an unnamed Creator to set up a government and pursue prosperity. The constitutional conventions and texts dictating the early formation of United States proclaim without reservation that white male landowners alone are commissioned into this new American reality. Thus the white American male becomes the ambassador of WAFR. Contrary to that decree, according to Christ, any repentant man, woman, or child reoriented to the risen Jesus becomes a son or daughter of the Most High God and an ambassador for his kingdom. These two missions and visions are not just incongruent, they are in opposition. With this vision at the core of the United States, it cannot be a Christian nation.

REPENTANCE AND RECONCILIATION

This became real to me as I sat in a Bible study reading 2 Corinthians 5. In December 2009, my wife, Priscilla, and I started dating, and the cultural narratives of our backgrounds were at play from our first meeting. On the surface I was black and she was Chinese and Korean. She was from the city; I was from a farm. She had gone south for college, and I came north for university. After college, she was immersed in Baltimore among people who looked like me, and my Christian fellowship and college experience was dominated by people who looked like her. The difference was that she was regularly willing to acknowledge and confess the places where she needed to learn and grow, and I was not. For years, when she pointed out my prejudice and bias, I dismissed her and became defensive. She could not reach me— but Jesus did one December day in 2016.

While engaging with this 2 Corinthians passage, I had to confess that when I sat with white and Asian people studying the Bible, I carried fear, suspicion, and judgment. When I sat in churches surrounded by those who didn't look like me, I was guarded in almost every way. I overexplained my thoughts because I feared being judged and misunderstood. I made sure to state my reasons for being present and detailed my accomplishments and qualifications. My primary goal was not to fulfill what I judged to be their stereotypes of me: black, male, angry, dangerous, and uneducated.

Moreover, I was suspicious when they shared traditionally liberal or conservative views, wondering what was on their reading lists, what podcasts they listened to, and what leaders developed and influenced them. I questioned whether they're "really Christians." I judged every word they said, parsing phrases to discern if they understood not just personal sin and salvation but God's plan for systemic redemption through Christ. I struggled to feel seen or heard and to trust them no matter how honest they were.

Jesus convicted me that December day. I had to confess that I can't stand to read, see, or value the leadership of prominent pastors such as Franklin Graham and Bill Johnson, who endorse Donald Trump's policies and make bigoted comments about police brutality that dismiss my brothers and sisters of color. I harbored bitterness and rage, and the longer time passed, my desire to love Johnson, Graham, and those like them faded.

My fear of being prejudged and misunderstood turned outward, and I judged, criticized, and condemned my brothers and sisters instead of genuinely engaging with them as people made in the image of God. Instead of embodying what I longed for, I perpetuated the thoughts and deeds I detested.

Underneath my fear of being misunderstood and judged is my fear of rejection. So I rejected others first. This is false power. My destructive fear was that if I fully showed up, gifts and faults included, I would be marginalized by those with money and power. So I cast myself to the edges of society before they had the chance to. At least then *I* chose my place. This is the twisted logic that prevents me from being reconciled to others, because I'm not fully reconciled to myself. And that most certainly holds reconciliation with God at bay.

Continuing to press in, I realized this was not only true in predominantly white and Asian spaces but with black and brown people as well. When I sat in pews filled by those who shared my skin, I assumed poverty and lack of resources. I immediately moved into messiah mode and thought of all I had to offer "these people." I took my internalized inferiority and projected it outward, crushing the image of God in my brothers and sisters because white supremacy crushed it in me. And instead of seeing God's abundance, I saw scarcity.

With an agenda in mind, I engaged with each person who shared my skin color and tried to decipher what their agenda might be. I was there to give, teach, and save. I felt validated and valuable in this role. In "my" community I had a part and must play it because if I didn't, I feared rejection again. So with each interaction there was an underlying question: *Is this an opportunity for us to move on up? To make it out?* When Jesus said of the religious leaders, "you blind guides" (Matthew 23:24), he is clearly talking about me. I criticized the American dream with one hand and offered it with the other. I spoke prophetically against exploitative capitalism out of one side of my mouth and tried to build my brand with the other. Jesus was the Savior for some, and the dollar was the messiah for others. I embodied the double-mindedness that broke my heart when I saw it at work in others.

Even more convicting than my pride and hypocrisy was that when I saw my non-Christian friends of any complexion or status, I kept up a wall of defense and silent judgment while waiting for a moment to invite them to Jesus. I was honest, but not too honest. I asked for input but didn't really value their advice.

Jesus was a friend to sinners. Thus, he was a friend to me. So why did I build fences and say I can't befriend those who don't follow Jesus?

I came to understand that extending forgiveness and choosing to love as Christ did does not minimize or dismiss the passive and active sins of racism, abuse, violence, misogyny, land theft, greed, or exploitative capitalism perpetrated and perpetuated by others toward me and marginalized communities. Nor does it minimize or dismiss the tragic trespasses committed against those in power. Confession and forgiveness is a proclamation that though people harm me, I will seek their health. Though they kill me, I will bless them. I will not yield to rage and wrath, but will be consumed by the ever-present love of God. Because those who are not yet reconciled to God know not the evil they do. So, as Jesus prayed for the soldier who pierced his side, I will pray for those who wish and do me harm. Not because their hatred doesn't matter, but because the love of God matters more. And because I have extended this grace, he extends grace and forgiveness to me (Matthew 6:14-15).

JESUS GOES FURTHER

This silent, personal confession to my personal Lord and Savior is where WAFR would have me stop. I would get a reward in the American church, but I am not complete in the kingdom until shalom reigns between me and those who have done me harm. Paul takes it up another level by pressing for the internal reorientation of our hearts, more commonly known as the repentance necessary to follow Jesus. Paul presses the external turns that transform our lives into windows for the kingdom of God and mirrors of Christlikeness. Thus, I had to sit before my Chinese-Korean American wife and confess the judgment that I held over her and her family. After five years of marriage, I had to ask for forgiveness and be reconciled to my wife for the ways I viewed her friends, family, and brothers and sisters in Christ. She extended grace and modeled for me what reconciliation should look like. Seeking shalom with our families and friendships across race, class, and status is hard, complicated work—but it is possible in Christ.

In Acts 2, Peter proclaims that the miracle of speaking in tongues was not alcohol induced but instead was the fulfillment of God's promise to pour out his Spirit on all people, male and female—and this is precisely what happened as foretold by the prophet Joel. People from all nations heard the word proclaimed in their own languages and were sent on mission for Jesus. In Acts 3 we read that Peter and the apostles continued to preach in power, heal the sick, and drive out demons. God's word went forth and did not return void but was accomplishing the purpose for which it was sent (Isaiah 55:11).

Jesus commissioned his followers to go forth and proclaim the good news, which was contrary to the mandate of Caesar and the Roman Empire. Historians of that day testified to what happened when the people of God responded not to the gods of the day but to Jesus by the power of the Holy Spirit. Julian the Apostate, the last pagan emperor of Rome, highlighted the countercultural witness of early Christians:

> These impious Galileans (Christians) not only feed their own, but ours also; welcoming them with their agape, they attract them, as children are attracted with cakes. . . . Whilst the pagan priests neglect the poor, the hated Galileans devote themselves to works of charity, and by a display of false compassion have established and given effect to their pernicious errors. Such practice is common among them, and causes contempt for our gods (Epistle to Pagan High Priests).[11]

Those in the early church lived in a conflicted but beloved covenant community in peaceful opposition to the militaristic, materialistic, racist, and sexualized culture of the Roman Empire. The church was distinct, noticeable, and uncompromising. This type of prayerful resistance and faithful witness is needed today.

Brandon and Faith Lee, who started Bird and Branch Coffee, are what faithful witnesses look like. When they sat down across from my wife and me, they had a dream to start a coffee shop that would serve as a place of refreshment and restoration. They wanted the planet, their employees, and all those who are a part of their supply chain, from producer to customer, to be better off because of their business.

It now exists for the flourishing of all, as God intended. They didn't hold the return on investment for their shareholders above the investment they were making in the laborers who harvest their beans, the baristas crafting each cup, or the planet's resources that make each drink and pastry possible. Brandon and Faith quit their jobs to ensure that those who lacked living wages and job training could have a shot at thriving in a society that says that they're unworthy because they once lived on the street, committed crimes, or were sexually exploited.

Brandon and Faith's parents did not come to America with the plan that their children would create jobs for the formerly homeless and incarcerated. That is not America's invitation and is certainly not the narrative for college-educated Chinese Americans living in New York City. But that is just one of the possibilities when two people fall in love with Jesus and choose the vision of the kingdom of God over the one offered by America. Their faithfulness is a reflection of a higher allegiance and an alternate citizenship that trumps the one that dominant culture and their family's history touts as superior.

Jesus' invitation into his redemptive life, death, and resurrection is at odds with pursuing pleasure at all costs. Even more apparent, a race-, class-, and gender-based hierarchy simply is not what Jesus preached. We discover in God's Word that selfish ambition for personal comfort and power is not the Great Commission. Living for oneself is not just inconsistent with Christianity, it's not Christian at all.

The lie that America is a Christian nation is dangerous because it distorts true Christian witness and the Great Commission to suit goals driven by idolatry. To claim that the United States is a Christian nation and that its citizens are by default Christian neutralizes the only population capable of sustaining a critique of empire—actual followers of Jesus. Because many self-proclaimed Christians exchange the mantle of truth and justice for the mantle of prosperity and political power, our hypocrisy compromises our integrity. And thus our lives bear witness to the kingdom of the world and not the kingdom of God.

When we have been drawn out of WAFR, we must be discipled into the new family of Jesus. We must draw distinct lines and make God's invitation crystal clear. The United States is rooted in genocide, land theft, institutionalized slave labor, and sexual exploitation. The kingdom of God is rooted in the sacrificial, transformative, and enduring love of God for all people. There are great promises and aspirations in the US Constitution, but it is neither a holy text nor does it describe the plan of God for the renewal of all creation and the restoration of shalom.

QUESTIONS FOR INDIVIDUAL REFLECTION AND SMALL GROUP DISCUSSION

- What were your dominant feelings as you read this chapter: fear confusion, numbness, familiarity, distance, or something else?

- Where in this chapter were these feelings the strongest?

- What phrases, stories, or historical events resonated with you? Where did you say, *Yes, that's it!*

- What events or narratives mentioned were you unaware of? What did you learn?

- Where do you disagree or have concerns? What questions are you carrying?

- Looking at Brandon and Faith's story, what did you find encouraging about the steps they took because of Jesus? What dream or vision do you have because of who Jesus has called us to be that might not align with the plans your family or society has for you?

BIBLE STUDY

Read through Acts 4 and reflect on or discuss the following questions.

- What practices and habits marked the religious authorities (rulers, elders, the teachers of the law, etc.)?

- Who were the religious authorities listening to and following? What about the apostles?

- What are the goals of the apostles and religious authorities?

- How do their goals conflict?

- Were their goals achieved?

- What practices from this Acts community can you integrate into your personal life and the life of your community?

LIE 2

WE ALL ARE IMMIGRANTS

DONALD TRUMP APPOINTED BEN CARSON as the Secretary for Housing and Urban Development in January 2017. On March 6, 2017, in Carson's first address to a room of federal workers under his leadership, he referred to African slaves as immigrants. His remarks, in context, were:

> That's what America is about. A land of dreams and opportunity. There were other immigrants who came here in the bottom of slave ships, worked even longer, even harder for less. . . . But they, too, had a dream that one day their sons, daughters, grandsons, granddaughters, great-grandsons, great-granddaughters might pursue prosperity and happiness in this land.[1]

As I read those words, I shook my head and tried to move on with my day. But instead I found myself on Twitter and Facebook, and following columnists for comments and dialogue. How could someone with dark skin stand in this country and say, "We are all immigrants"?

I was angry.

But I had to ask myself what was under the anger. That was more difficult to determine.

I was angry because I remember my father's voice trailing off when he told me about the first Ku Klux Klan rally he saw. In 1959, he was nine years old, and Prince Edward County, Virginia, refused to integrate its schools. One late afternoon, as he walked home, he saw a crowd of white men across a field light a cross on fire. Crosses took on a very different purpose in his young mind. Next to that cross was a Confederate flag, and though he was transfixed by these images, he ran away for fear of being lynched if he were seen. This is my history. This is the history of my family and neighbors—those terrified by the burning cross and those who lit it on fire. This is also the history of the United States.

According to Merriam-Webster, an immigrant is someone from one country who comes to make permanent residence in another. This implies that the person arriving does so willingly, if not enthusiastically. This belief, along with white American folk religion's view of history, paints slaves and those fleeing war, genocide, religious persecution, poverty, violence, and natural disasters with the same broad brush. It's depressingly simple to say everyone in this country came to seek better economic opportunities. This fits WAFR's narrative. This lie, more than any other of the twelve lies that hold America captive, is attractive because of our culture's unwillingness and inability to engage in difficult conversations about pain and suffering. The second lie, that *we are all immigrants*, obviously avoids the past. And it conveniently allows those who have experienced or inflicted present or historical trauma to move forward.

This outworking of WAFR encourages white Southerners to think that the Confederate flag is about Southern pride and culture, not a symbol of oppression and violence. It is why the slogan Make America Great Again resonates so strongly with one demographic but confuses and frightens others. It is why Chinese, Filipino, and Dominican American students often are unaware that their parents came to this country illegally and they themselves are undocumented until they find out when applying for college. WAFR forcefully and falsely suggests that "we're all the same." But we never have been nor will we ever be. WAFR will not bring that reality about; nor is it what God intended.

After a time of lament and prayer because of Carson's words, I realized that feelings of shock, disappointment, and fear lay under my anger.

SHOCK

I was shocked because I cannot remember a day in which I was not conscious of my racial assignment as black and that my ancestors were slaves. I was reminded by warnings from my mom, comments in school or at work, and casual-turned-intense conversations informing me that I should "stay with my own kind." To the world around me, I am black. And to respond with "I don't see color" dismisses my lived experience. I invite whites to consider what your parents, grandparents, aunts, and uncles might say if you adopted an African American son or married someone of my ethnic background. Their reactions might not reflect the kingdom of God but might represent the state of things in a land dominated by white supremacy and the anti-Christian outworking of WAFR.

The words of a teammate on my high school soccer team ring in my head to this day, "You're not like those other n———s, Walton. You're a good one!" Perhaps it was a twisted compliment, like a catcall that's meant to empower but just demeans and dehumanizes. I'm a *good one*. I never did get to ask him what he meant by it because the whistle blew and practice began. Moving forward in the midst of so much unprocessed pain is tragic but expected by those who inhabit the margins. We are to carry our pain like coins that no one accepts as currency anymore.

Like Ben Carson, I am Ivy League educated. And if attending an elite university as a black male in 2004 was a struggle, no doubt the hurdles for him at Yale were glaringly visible some decades ago. Ethnic minorities feel a sense of comfort when someone like *us* rises to a place of influence and leadership. So I was surprised and disappointed by what he said. Similar to when Barack Obama was elected, I held out hope that something redemptive would arise. This hope is unfounded because redemption is only possible through Christ. That being true, Carson's statement was not a hard pill to swallow but a fist-size stone I was force-fed. I did not want to accept that this is where *we* are.

FEAR

After the shock, I was gripped by fear. What policies would Carson create, promote, and put into place that would negatively affect communities of color across the country? What lies would be peddled to women and men who need help with food, housing, and equal opportunities in education? How many generations would be kept in cycles of poverty because of deals marketed as "good for the inner city" but actually eliminate affordable housing and drive impoverished people into further instability? How are we going to address the rising numbers of poor white Americans in post-industrial suburbs and rural towns ravaged by opioid abuse and lack of opportunity?

I feel shock and fear every time I hear those in political power cast a vision of *freedom*, *justice*, and *equality* rooted in lies, greed, and self-interest.

DISAPPOINTMENT

Then disappointment emerged because personal and corporate suffering does not ease with time but instead becomes normalized. And because of my self- and social awareness, I am not able to overcome the fear of potential abuse of power that could come at any moment. Slavery, colonization, war, and social and economic exclusion affect every people group that came or was brought to America as well as those natives already here. The stress and trauma of that history are amplified when the lies, greed, and self-interest are veiled behind Holy Scripture taken out of context and professed as an act of faithful service to Christ.

My unsettledness finds its fault line here. Carson and other American evangelical leaders appear to be faithful not to the crucified Christ but to the powers of this world that nailed Jesus to the cross. This play for political power and dismissal of biblical integrity is epitomized by Tony Perkins, the head of the Family Research Council, when he said that President Trump gets a "mulligan" on sexual assault, adultery, and his chronic objectification of women.[2] This dialogue was sparked by the emergence of Trump's extramarital affair with Stephanie Clifford, also known as Stormy Daniels. This is called good strategy or political pragmatism by pundits and journalists analyzing Christian leaders' endorsements and partnerships with those in positions of power. White evangelical pastors publicly weigh Supreme Court nominations and socially conservative legal "wins" against the cost of condemning Trump's behavior. Their calculus might be savvy in political science, but from the perspective of Scripture, it is idolatry.

The joining of WAFR and the powers of the world, espoused as an exercise of God's holy power, is constant and problematic. This was true when the Pharisees and Sadducees aligned with the Roman Empire for wealth, power, and status. This was true of the Catholic Church as their missionaries accompanied the military and merchants in the conquest of what is now the Americas.

The conquering of native peoples as *manifest destiny* and the myth of America as "God's country" creates an unbiblical theology of the state that aims to change the definition of who God is and how followers are to worship him. This religious and social reorganization makes government leaders not just God-ordained but into deities themselves. Thus the ordinances and laws these morally superior humans create move from being policies to divinely inspired ways of life. Consequently, with the false god defined, the next step is to provide a common story for its worshipers. WAFR redefines Jesus, then attempts to redefine us by proclaiming *we are all immigrants*.

The lie that we are all immigrants aims to determine who we are by altering how we see our own history and the histories of those around us. What happened, who did it, and why it occurred is not as important as moving forward and what's possible now. This invitation to a "clean slate" and a "common story" softens the soil of our hearts for the seeds of tempting dishonesty that are about to be planted. It is a beautiful lie to live out of a false, affirming past. To simply overlook or reimagine that the blood flowing through my veins does not come from the children of parents who were raped, abused, and enslaved is destructive and impossible. It would be a profound denial for me to wake up each day and not be part of a people whose bodies were thrown off ships after dying in their own feces or branded on arrival. It would be equally untrue to believe the people who committed genocide, held whips, locked chains, and bred God's image bearers like cattle were mere immigrants working hard for a better life and not the creators, sustainers, perpetrators, and victims of a distorted system of white supremacy.

The whites of our world are the first victims of white supremacy. This system punishes all who are involved in it, including those who benefit from it: the Dutch, Germans, British, French, Polish, Irish, Italians, and all others who pass for white in today's America. They faced varying levels of suspicion, hostility, and claims of inferiority, and had to create, adopt, and enforce the "we are all immigrants" lie to achieve and maintain social inclusion. No group is exempt from the damage wrought by colonization and systemic oppression—even those in power.

The next victims of this ideology, after those who perpetrated the lie, were native people. The natives who lived in the mid-Atlantic region of America were not immigrants but inhabitants with vibrant cultures, customs, and practices. These indigenous people were not savages but members of families and complex communities of God-given worth. My Cherokee great-grandmother loved music and long walks. The Trail of Tears, which the Cherokee people faced beginning in the 1830s, was a death march, and socioeconomic isolation or forced assimilation awaited those who survived this terrible journey.

WAFR fosters forgetting and then propagates an edited retelling of the narrative in a way that affirms the powerful and assimilates the powerless into a lower position in the power structure. For example, the supposedly Christian boarding schools attempted to crush native identities in many tribes (there were twenty-three tribes represented in one Phoenix Boarding School).[3] This was done by physically and culturally separating native children from their elders and forbidding them to speak their tribal language. Over time the children became unaware of their ethnic identity. They had to ask white American men who they were.

The lie that we are a nation of immigrants whitewashes history and constructs a narrative that keeps the powerful and the powerless from reflecting, confessing, repenting, and seeking justice and shalom. The privilege of moving on is a hallmark of WAFR that stands in profound opposition to the Hebrew prophets and Jesus' disciples. Yet social forgetting is necessary in order to center ourselves and our purposes on the world and not on the risen Jesus, which is precisely what WAFR invites all to do.

REFLECTION AND REMEMBRANCE

In Joshua 4, we see Moses' successor leading the Hebrew people through the desert and into the Promised Land. The Hebrew people experienced four hundred years of slavery, and their leader survived the state-sanctioned murder of a generation of his brothers. They were an ethnic group who suffered violence, abuse, and death while building structures to Egyptian idols.[4] Once liberated from the pharaoh, these women, men, and children wandered the desert for forty years and watched a generation of those who only knew slavery pass away without seeing the Promised Land (Joshua 5:4-6). Simultaneously, these people knew God's provision as they received manna daily from heaven, their shoes did not wear out, and miraculous events brought about their freedom from Egypt (Exodus 16; Nehemiah 9). They knew they were a chosen people set apart by God (Deuteronomy 7:6) to be consecrated for his glory. These were people marked by great oppression and privilege, by lack and provision.

These narratives weren't merely passed on to the children over meals and long walks; they were also told through marks on bodies that bore the scars of forced labor and the mental anguish of slavery. These memories had tastes, smells, feelings, and sounds. In hindsight, I'm guessing that the people would rather not have some of these memories, but they nevertheless probably cherished their collective memory. From our context it would be tempting not to look back but only to the future. After all, the promise is so much better than the past. But to the Israelites, the past was as indispensable as the present and future.

In Joshua 4:1-18 we read an account of the Israelites on the banks of the Jordan River. Like Moses, Joshua faces a body of water and must cross it with the people of God by the power of God. It is practical and significant—practical because the Jordan flows between them and the Promised Land, and spiritually significant because of its parallel to the story of Moses. If history was dismissed or rewritten, then the significance of this moment would be lost. But reflection and remembrance are essential parts of their culture. The book of Joshua opens with the death of Moses and blessed reassurance that the presence and power of God would go with Joshua as long as he was strong and courageous (Joshua 1:1-7). He is promised success in battle and the allegiance of the people as long as he holds fast to what is right and true.

> No man will [be able to] stand before you [to oppose you] as long as you live. Just as I was [present] with Moses, so will I be with you; I will not fail you or abandon you. Be strong *and* confident and courageous, for you will give this people as an inheritance the land which I swore to their fathers (ancestors) to give them. Only be strong and very courageous; be careful to do [everything] in accordance with the entire law which Moses My servant commanded you; do not turn from it to the right or to the left, so that you may prosper *and* be successful wherever you go. (Joshua 1:5-7 AMP)

God's people received promises and see the fulfillment of those promises. Joshua is called to meditate and reflect on God's law and promises so that he might be faithful and obedient. That is the reason he is reflective, submissive, and able to walk in the power and authority of God. The sequence of hearing from God, reflecting on what he says, and walking in obedience are marks of Hebrew prophetic leadership.

Moreover, in Joshua 4 these rhythms are not only for certain people but also for all people. God commands Joshua to instruct one representative from each of the twelve tribes to select a stone from the river to be used to create a monument of memory (vv. 21-24). Though this new generation never cut stones for idols or suffered under Pharaoh, they would cut stones and carry them to be an altar unto the one true God. This practice of collective memory stands in direct conflict with the tenets of WAFR. Joshua and the people of God hold their oppression and freedom, liberation and slavery, and promise and fulfillment in beautiful tension. American culture is unwilling and unable to do that, which stands in opposition to the remembrance, reflection, and reconciliation necessary in the kingdom of God. The Israelites did not dismiss their history and culture for the sake of comfort and conflict avoidance. They lived out the identity given to them by God.

My people were not immigrants in search of a better life, they were slaves brought to this country. They were stripped of their names, identities, and futures, and given ones that suited others' purposes. Made in the image of God, they were never meant to be slaves. Remembering and reflecting is part of every culture, but it does not serve the aims of WAFR. I know none of the names of the British slave owners whose blood fills my veins; that lack of connection is intentional. Family trees in fairer-skinned households of southern Virginia don't include people who look like me.

Furthermore, when I dialogue with my Chinese-Korean mother-in-law, who came to this country fleeing institutional racism, the term *immigrant* feels insufficient. The same is true for my wife's childhood friend who came here from Ghana shortly after his uncles were murdered and his father was going to be next. Moreover, this feeling of insufficiency is true for my friends from the Southwestern United States, where the border shifted beneath their elders' feet and all of a sudden they were Americans. These people trust me with their stories; they are children of war, poverty, violence, and ethnic prejudice. They didn't leave their country because it was inherently inferior to America.

They left because they were kicked out, threatened, or lacked the resources to thrive in their own context.

My Korean grandmother sharing that she knows what burning flesh smells like in the midst of war, and my Salvadoran friend's recounting having to decide which of his siblings would walk across the desert to earn money for medical treatment for their sick mother—these are not just unfortunate stories. They are tragedies of the human condition where military, economic, and geopolitical policy are devastating—and America is often complicit, if not the sole destabilizing factor.

Into this devastation comes the resurrected Jesus with the power to redeem, reconcile, and commission. He adopts us—the broken and those who do the breaking—into the family of God and says we are made righteous through his sacrifice. Jesus proclaims, "Blessed are the peacemakers" (Matthew 5:9), not the peacekeepers. With his love and acceptance at the center, he has made peace with us, so we can enter into the pain, struggle, and brokenness perpetrated against us and that we perpetrate against others. The love of Christ compels us to press in, and he holds all things together. Instead of being broken by sharing these stories, my Korean grandmother is able to grow closer to the youngest generation of her family. (Her stories are recorded for posterity via Story Corps.) My brother from El Salvador testifies to the faithfulness of God, and the body of Christ is encouraged to love fully and see the undocumented through the eyes of Jesus. Neither they nor I are broken by our histories, but we feel increasingly seen, heard, and known the more we share.

Contrary to the call of Christ, WAFR offers an alternate narrative: "Let's not remember. Let's do something different. Let's be someone different." Though this frame of mind is tempting, it is dishonest and a destructive proposition, as we must never exchange the truth for a lie.

IDENTITY IN THE KINGDOM OF GOD

In order to achieve the new identity offered by WAFR, we must earn and maintain it. We orient our lives around creating "our best lives now," seeking what suits our personal comfort and self-determined best interests. And only if we "make it" can we then start to help those around us to do the same thing. This narrative of "work hard to gain possessions, wealth, influence, and social status to ensure comfort and avoid suffering" is far from what it looks like to be a faithful follower of Jesus.

Instead, Christ invites us to receive an identity already earned by him. I saw the struggle between these two realities in the eyes of my wife, Priscilla, in 2014. She was contemplating a $25,000 per year pay cut and a professional step backward if she decided to leave school leadership and head back to the classroom. This would also be a step off the fast track to opening her own school in New York City in exchange for working at arguably the most influential charter school network in the country. Two circumstances sparked this transition. First, an email from one of her supervisors—"If you're not anxious, you're not doing your job"—captured the toxic and suffocating culture around her. She was being developed as a leader, but this was not the type of person she wanted to be. Second, her father had terminal cancer, and she wanted to spend time reconciling that relationship during the last months of his life. This wasn't just a choice between working less to spend more time with family. It was a choice between an identity grounded in an idol that would ultimately destroy her or being rooted in Christ and having an unshakable foundation.

Priscilla chose obedience to Christ and to honor boundaries that would lead to her flourishing, not idolatry that would produce more anxiety, striving, and burnout. In the context of WAFR and the pursuit of comfort and status at all costs, it makes no sense for a second-generation Chinese-Korean American to take a pay cut and a lower position in the power structure of her field. But to a daughter of the Most High God, whose identity will never change, the choice is still difficult but clear. She followed Jesus, left that job, and truly lacks nothing.

The call of Christ is an invitation to receive an identity already earned for us. Instead of being invited to a party where we work for our seat at the table, we are told our place is paid for and cannot be lost or taken by someone else. I am not a worker but a son, and my sisters are daughters who have a permanent place at the Creator's table. The child with Down syndrome and the CEO of a multinational corporation are of equal worth, and men and women are on level ground. Paul affirms this reality:

> You are all sons of God through faith in Christ Jesus. For all of you who were baptized into Christ have clothed yourselves with Christ. There is neither Jew nor Greek, there is neither slave nor free man, there is neither male nor female; for you are all one in Christ Jesus. And if you belong to Christ, then you are Abraham's descendants, heirs according to promise. (Galatians 3:26-29)

The parable in Luke 14:16-24 illustrates the choice between entering into the presence of God and prioritizing earthly relationships and material possessions. A man invited many friends to a feast. But they all rejected his offer. So he invited the city's outcasts, who willingly came. This parable illustrates the clear choice Jesus' listeners had. They could spend time with Jesus or do something else. It also shows us what God's reaction is to the rejection of his invitation. The head of the household does not become angry and cancel his banquet. He doesn't send messengers again to share his disappointment and heap shame or guilt on them to get them to come. He doesn't scold them or threaten to end their friendships. Neither does he use social, familial, or political power to force those invited to attend. He says instead, "Go, ask other people." This speaks to the nature of the Christian God, who, though jealous for our affection, will not hold us captive.

Some of the "friends" are concerned with their possessions. They choose to tend to the home or apartment they just purchased with all of their savings, or testing and cleaning the new vehicle they now own. Another prioritizes a relationship with his spouse over an invitation from Jesus. As every romantic movie suggests, and as I know from my own experiences, those in romantic relationships and close friendships often choose to cultivate those relationships rather than give time and attention to their relationship with God.

Aren't these the very things that WAFR promises to those who buy into the "we are all immigrants" story line, willing to run the race for life, liberty, and happiness? This false Christianity sees winners as those who reach for the American dream and orient their best efforts to have the best possible romantic partner and most material possessions. Conversely, winners in true Christianity are those willing to lose their lives in Christ and gain all they will ever need.

BELONGING TO A LARGER COMMUNITY

Systematically oppressed minority and marginalized groups often band together for safety, comfort, and a sense of belonging. The social isolation that marginalization brings can lead to a strong community and commitments to support one another. At its best, we witness marvelous compassion and generosity in times of need among immigrant families. They welcome newcomers and offer them food, shelter, employment, and community. Sometimes, though, fear, suspicion, and ethnocentrism drive minorities to see other people groups as threats and only to be engaged if they are useful.

When Priscilla and I prayerfully decided that we should get married, we had to overcome serious cultural barriers. Prejudice between the Chinese and Korean communities and African Americans is not imaginary. I had few experiences with anyone from Asia before coming to college. Television, pop culture, and pornography shaped my opinions of Korean and Chinese people—all of which are tragic misrepresentations and appropriations of a rich, beautiful, and diverse people.

Priscilla knew people of nearly every nation from growing up in the New York borough of Queens, but her perception of Southern African Americans was warped as well. It was difficult for her to find an acceptable perspective, so she did her best to make no assumptions and simply ask questions. Our parents' perceptions were worse; the Chinese and Korean communities were often redlined into living and working in neighborhoods with African Americans. Suspicion, fear, and violence marked these interactions. Priscilla warned me that her family members might not speak to me because the only interactions they had with men and women who looked like me were during business or burglaries.

My wife is the daughter of immigrants who fled political persecution and discrimination in their native lands. To say they were looking for a better life is a laughable understatement. They left to live.

It was a real possibility that members of her family would not speak to her if she married me. Why? Because it would violate deep values and beliefs. Much like the Israelites, their identities are tied to history, culture, and the collective. So it was not just her family but also others in the Chinese and Korean communities that might ostracize her.

Practically, this would mean no holiday parties, wedding invitations, or updates on new babies or older family members passing away. It would mean no inheritance or naming of our children by her elders. Names carry significant weight in Priscilla's family and culture. Embedded in Priscilla's name are centuries of history and significance. The written character of her family name, Pan, can be traced back hundreds of years. She shares Jia, her generational name, with all of her cousins on that side of her family. The name is lifted from one line of an epic poem that determines that generation's common name and character. The last portion, En, is her given name, chosen by her grandparents. Priscilla may be her English name, and she is seen as an individual by Western culture, but in her culture individuality is not prized or sought after. Those in her ethnic community are instead joined to a beautiful collective. Thus her family members call her not by her name but by her relationship to them. For example, her only sibling calls her Jie or "older sister," and only her niece calls her Da Gu Ma. Her mother and father call her Xiao-En or "Little Grace," a term of endearment that no one else will use.

This focus on relationships implies that Priscilla is her family and her family is her.

For Priscilla, marrying me would not only violate her cultural narrative, it would also violate a tenet of WAFR because marrying a black male would move Priscilla and her children down the social ladder. For generations to come, this would set back their pursuit of life, liberty, and happiness because of their diverse heritage, darker skin, and presumably poor, dangerous, and uneducated black father.

Against this backdrop, Priscilla prayed to the God who raised Jesus from the dead. During this season of discernment, a time she set aside to hear from God and others about whether she should marry me, she saw a vision of Jesus. She and I were walking hand in hand in his presence. The choice for her became clear. She could pursue the comfort, stability, and security of her family and culture or live in obedience to Jesus. She chose to follow Jesus and a marriage dedicated to him and his purposes. She decided to marry me.

After Priscilla shared this vision with her parents, they relented and enthusiastically gave me a name—Jonathan Jia-Sheng Pan Walton. It carries connotations of a warm and welcoming home (Jia) along with imagery of a rising sun (Sheng). I too became part of the family with my generational name, my given name, and my family name. Tears filled my eyes the first time I was called son and stood for a family photo. My father-in-law proclaimed, "I need a picture with my sons." I had been adopted! The love of Jesus had triumphed over fear.

The collective identity of her family and culture married to WAFR created an anti-Christian cocktail that passes as authentic Christianity in ethnic-specific churches all over the United States and in other countries. Congregations fend for their members' everyday needs, and because of oppression, they gather in faith communities that are actually social clubs and support groups punctuated by Bible studies and occasional encounters with God. Sunday morning services and midweek meetings function as supportive spaces for folks of the same racial assignment who seek upward mobility or wider influence. This is not to say that ethnic-specific churches are not honoring to God and don't have faithful expressions of witness to Jesus. I am saying that in the context of the United States, under the banner of white supremacy, myths of the "model minority," and deep race and class segregation, what passes for radical and rooted faith has an unbiblical low bar.

My wife and I are descendants of a complex collection of people made in the image of God. We desperately need his reconciliation and shalom—peace in all relationships—as we live in this country. And opting out of the "we are all immigrants" myth from WAFR allows us to live into the gospel and mission of Jesus (2 Corinthians 5). Our marriage, possessions, bank account, and social status are not testimonies to our own hard work or that "America works," but to the faithfulness of Christ and the work he is doing in the world. The everyday hope and prayer I have for our daughter, Maia Pan Bang Jie Walton, is not that she would move up the social ladder and attain unprecedented levels of wealth, comfort, and stability. I pray that the days would be short between now and when she knows God as her good Father; commits to Jesus as her Lord, Savior, King, and Friend; and is filled with the Holy Spirit.

My family's liberation and the subsequent freedom does not mean we forget what came before us. On the contrary, we name it and praise Jesus for how far his freedom has brought us. Otherwise, we will be tempted to repeat the empty pursuit of creating our own identity when we already have one from God.

QUESTIONS FOR INDIVIDUAL REFLECTION AND SMALL GROUP DISCUSSION

- What were your dominant feelings as you read this chapter: curiosity, hope, surprise, confusion, numbness, familiarity, distance, or something else?

- Where were those feelings most present?

- What phrases, stories, or historical events resonated with you?

- What events or narratives were you unaware of? What did you learn?

- Where do you disagree or have concerns?

- What questions are you carrying?

GET TO KNOW YOURSELF AND OTHERS MORE DEEPLY

Answer the following questions and share your responses with others:

- What are the significant events that mark your family? Perhaps a revolution or war brought your family to another country, or a job opportunity for your grandmother changed your family's narrative. Identify three to five important events that made a lasting impact.

- Turn to the "Where I'm From" poem exercise in appendix 1. Upload a video to your favorite social media platform like Facebook, Instagram, or Twitter and share it with our community using #12Lies.

- Turn to the Ethnic Identity Interview in appendix 2. It is impossible to interact with someone and not engage with their history. This is a chance to get to know your friends and family!

LIE 3

WE ARE A MELTING POT

I GREW UP IN BRODNAX, VIRGINIA, on a road where my mother's family has lived for more than a century. The town has about four hundred people, and my house didn't show up on Google Maps when it launched in 2005. The closest big town of about four thousand is South Hill. They have the Walmart.

There were no neighborhoods in Brodnax, as my young mind understood them at the time. I thought, *If you can't see the house next to you, like on TV, then that's not a neighborhood.* But South Hill was different. They had Circle Drive and Fox Run, along with Pettus Town and Chaptico Road. Most important was not that I knew where they were but that I knew who belonged there. Even the smallest towns in America had versions of redlining, a complex set of discriminatory housing practices that included mortgage lending, insurance rates, and other financial and social means to keep races and classes apart. Circle Drive and Fox Run were for black folks, and Pettus Town and Chaptico Road were for white people with "old money." *Old money* refers to the money, land, wealth, and resources these people possessed because of colonization, slavery, and institutional racism. These resources were obtained at the expense of the slaves they owned, their advantages gained through the benefits of Jim Crow, or racial discrimination in education, housing, and financing. These resources and statuses were kept in place by acts of violence like threats and verbal intimidation along with lynching, police brutality, cross burnings, and murders.

By sixteen I was familiar with this way of life. They weren't theories or ideas, but stories I heard and experiences I had. I'll never forget arguing with the mom of one of my best friend's in her kitchen. They were white and lived on Chaptico Road. She told me they wanted to send their daughter to Kenston Forest, a private school. In my mind that meant one thing: people went to private schools in southern Virginia to get away from "bad behavior," the "wrong crowd," and "negative influences." To me that meant getting away from black people and potential "race mixing." God forbid a white girl take a black boy to prom or a black woman marry a white man. In 1967, *Loving v. Virginia* made interracial marriage legal, but you could still be beaten or killed for "mixing."[1] I knew that public money, including taxes paid by black folks, helped start these private schools during integration.[2] I knew that "more opportunities" and "better classroom management" meant no blacks and no poor people. I knew this at sixteen years old but could articulate none of it. After all, what was I doing in a house on Chaptico Road anyway—if I wasn't cutting the grass? So, this little girl left her middle school to head off to Kenston Forest, and I went back home to Allen Road. Unfortunately, this was and is not only a Southern problem. The *New York Times* points out that the entire country shared a common ethos of racial segregation, especially in education.[3]

Around the same time, my girlfriend went to study at the home of one of her classmates. She is black and he is white; he lived in Pettus Town. His mother, who taught my younger brother in middle school, asked him to come into another room. She proceeded to tell him, loud enough for my girlfriend to hear, that he "should have never brought a n—— in her house." What were people going to think? What would the neighbors say? So, he came out with his head down and drove her home.

The perception of America might be that we're a melting pot, but common belief, wisdom, and practice is that some folks aren't supposed to have friendships with, date, marry, or even go to church with people of another race, ethnicity, or socioeconomic background. This isn't limited to black and white people, though it's the most socially egregious. Personally, I've watched the prejudice and hatred pour out between the parents and potential spouses of Chinese and Filipino couples: "You know, they're like the Mexicans of Asian people, Jonathan." I've heard more explicit instructions that immigrant parents give their children to maintain their "purity," especially their daughters: "Here's the list of people that my [Chinese] grandfather told me I could marry: Chinese, Cambodian, Korean, Thai, Laos, Filipino, Japanese, white, or Latino." And I've heard comments that are vague but wound just as deeply: "I would want you to marry someone Korean because it's just . . . easier."

I've never heard someone say that black men are preferable for marriage—even from those who share my skin color from a place of wholeness. These comments are painful. And white American folk religion will work to ensure that marriage between ethnically or racially different people never actually happens.

THE MYTH OF THE MELTING POT

A melting pot is used during the process of heating metal to obtain purified ore. For example, to make bronze, one has to melt tin and copper and then combine them. The metal is heated in order to strain out what the metal worker doesn't want and then the pure tin and copper come together to produce bronze. Specifically, for copper smelting, a crucible must be used. In smelting, two purified elements come together under intense heat to produce one completely different compound. Bronze is neither copper nor tin but a different substance altogether that takes the best from both.

The term *melting pot* as applied to social life appeared in the eighteenth and nineteenth centuries and was used to describe the diverse mosaic taking shape in America. The idea was popularized and effective. It made the United States seem like a promised land where folks could live together in unity. Not only that, but the melting pot image also projected a wonderful prospect where many people come together to form a unique and better people. *E pluribus unum* (one out of many) captures that ideal so perfectly that it appears on every coin.

It is a wonderful motto except for the fact that it's contrary to the vision of the world God intended and will bring to pass. Early American leaders worked to make the melting pot a reality. Conversely, we see in Revelation 7 how and why their vision is woefully inadequate and not grounded in the word of God.

A speech that came to be called "Kill the Indian, and Save the Man" was delivered at George Mason University in 1892 by Captain Richard Pratt. The caption under a photo of him notes him to be the "Father of the Movement in Getting Indians Out from Their Old Life to Citizenship." This is accurate because he was the founder of the Carlisle Indian Industrial Schools, one of the many oppressive, abusive, and violent places where Native American boys and girls were cruelly forced to assimilate.

Pratt's remarks began,

> A great general has said that the only good Indian is a dead one, and that high sanction of his destruction has been an enormous factor in promoting Indian massacres. In a sense, I agree with the sentiment, but only in this: that all the Indian there is in the race should be dead. Kill the Indian in him, and save the man.
>
> We are just now making a great pretense of anxiety to civilize the Indians. I use the word "pretense" purposely, and mean it to have all the significance it can possibly carry. Washington believed that commerce freely entered into between us and the Indians would bring about their civilization, and Washington was right. He was followed by Jefferson, who inaugurated the reservation plan. Jefferson's reservation was to be the country west of the Mississippi; and he issued instructions to those controlling Indian matters to get the Indians there, and let the Great River be the line between them and the whites. Any method of securing removal—persuasion, purchase, or force— was authorized. Jefferson's plan became the permanent policy. The removals have generally been accomplished by purchase, and the evils of this are greater than those of all the others combined.[4]

He continues to explain how melting *together* was never the intention, but an explicit melting *into* would be more accurate. He used enslavement of Africans as his lens for how to deal with Native Americans. After explaining that all of the United States should come under the rule of God, the Declaration of Independence, and the Constitution, he claims that slavery was a blessing to the seven million Africans taken from "cannibalism in the darkest Africa" to enlightened America. The great lesson of slavery as he sees it is:

> The schools did not make them [slaves] citizens, the schools did not teach them the language, nor make them industrious and self-supporting. Denied the right of schools, they became English-speaking and industrious through the influences of association. Scattered here and there, under the care and authority of individuals of the higher race, they learned self-support and something of citizenship, and so reached their present place. No other influence or force would have so speedily accomplished such a result. Left in Africa, surrounded by their fellow-savages, our seven million of industrious black fellow-citizens would still be savages. Transferred into these new surroundings and experiences, behold the result. They became English-speaking and civilized, because forced into association with English-speaking and civilized people; became healthy and multiplied, because they were property; and industrious, because industry, which brings contentment and health, was a necessary quality to increase their value.

What he explains is less of a melting pot and more a filter that strains out what the dominant culture finds undesirable. Pratt's remarks twist Scripture, and linking forced submission to a god defined by those in power with support for America's core beliefs and actions. Consequently, all people who live in America and under its social, political, economic, and military influence have two choices: either resist, and thus exist, on the outside of this system at its

mercy, or enter into this common story of WAFR. Those who assimilate begin the race to pursue life, liberty, and happiness, beginning where the starting line is determined by racial assignment,
social class, gender, and status. This includes and is also true for
those society considers white.

Oppression, discrimination, and racism press American community to assimilate or force them to turn inward for protection. As
InterVarsity student leader Katie McCarty observed, "We are less of a
melting pot and more of a buffet. We are together, but we don't touch."

What WAFR prescribes is "assimilate or die." If not literal death,
then certainly it produces a disadvantaged life: a person or group of
people who refuses to assimilate or is prevented from assimilating is
forced into American society's silos, such as reservations, ghettos, internment camps, and prisons.

Racial hierarchy based on gender and skin color is married to false
religious ideas and receives moral justification. The following passage
from *American Crucible* by Cambridge professor Gary Gerstle explains
the melding of cultures into one superior identity:

> Understand that America is God's Crucible, the great Melting-Pot
> where all the races of Europe are melting and re-forming! Here
> you stand, good folk, think I, when I see them at Ellis Island,
> here you stand in your fifty groups, your fifty languages, and
> histories, and your fifty blood hatreds and rivalries. But you
> won't be long like that, brothers, for these are the fires of God
> you've come to—these are fires of God. A fig for your feuds and
> vendettas! Germans and Frenchmen, Irishmen and Englishmen,
> Jews and Russians—into the Crucible with you all! God is
> making the American.[5]

The end result is not a place where every ethnicity and culture receive
space to flourish and be celebrated; instead, all cultures yield to "the
will of God" and become American, because that is certainly his will.
But examining Scripture, we see that a melting pot is not God's plan.

GOD'S KINGDOM IS NOT A MELTING POT

Even if America were able to achieve a perfect blending of each ethnic identity and racial group into one social image that embodies *e pluribus unum*, that would fall short of God's vision revealed to the apostle John in Revelation 7:9-17. In this passage, the people gathered before the throne of God are not white people and black people or those forced to forget their distinctive ethnocultural identities by checking boxes like Asian, Hispanic, Native American, or Other.

In China and Korea, people don't self-identify as Asian. There are dozens of ethnic groups in those countries. There are no Hispanics in South America or Pacific Islanders in Tonga and Samoa. Even those nations and islands are identified by names given to them, not the ones they used for themselves. On the land where I grew up and the soil under Columbia University where I studied, people groups rich in culture, tradition, and beauty once resided and were dispossessed and displaced.

These categories were created in America and places where white supremacy, racism, and ethnocentrism reign. These categories were instituted and are kept in place only while a dominant culture seeks to elevate itself and subjugate others.

In the kingdom of God people are not forced to fit into a racial hierarchy for the sake of easy classification, control, or exploitation. The kingdom of God is not a melting pot. Those gathered before the throne of God in Revelation 7 are precisely where they are supposed to be without having to *code switch* or translate their mother tongues. They are at home in front of the God who always intended them to be with him. They are also at home with one another and all those in the multiethnic body of Christ.

This is not every tribe, tongue, and nation assimilating into a singular culture. If it were a large, diverse group of people now speaking the same language and sharing the same culture and heritage, John could have specified that, but the Greek words chosen reveal shalom amid difference: *nations*, *tribes*, *peoples*, and *tongues*.

Luis Bush, an Argentinian-born, Singaporean-based leader in global Christianity notes:

The emphasis of these combinations is on completeness, totality, fullness . . . γλῶσσα (glossa) in the Revelation passages emphasizes people as a linguistic unity and is the Greek term that best expresses ethno linguistic peoples. In conclusion, as we consider the four synonyms used in the Bible related to peoples, the term ἔθνος (ethnos) relates to ethno cultural peoples as distinct from *ethno* linguistic peoples, γλῶσσα (glossa) or ethno political peoples, λαός (laos) or φυλή (phylē) which refers to people as a national unity of common descent.[6]

This is a place where striving ceases and provision flows abundantly. This is not a place where ethnic groups are pitted against each other like the sugar plantations of Hawaii. This is not a place where lightness or darkness of skin determines your treatment as on the tobacco farms of southern Virginia. Heaven is perfect peace in the presence of God with the people of God, including our ethnic identity, language, and culture. These things are given by God and pleasing to him when we consecrate them to his glory. They were not meant to be squeezed out of us by oppression, violence, or the lack of education, wealth, or social mobility.

The rejection of WAFR and the embrace of the kingdom of God beautifully reconciled under the reign of Jesus Christ reminds me of standing on the floor of the Edward Jones Dome at the Urbana 06 Student Missions Conference in St. Louis. InterVarsity Christian Fellowship hosts this triennial conference where twenty thousand mostly college students gather to contemplate the call of Christ and take prayerful, practical action in response to Jesus. There were nearly as many people there as live in Mecklenburg County, where I grew up. I was nineteen and had never attended a Christian conference. All assumptions I had were shattered when I arrived. This was not a Christian concert! It was not a collection of famous Christians I'd never heard of and motivational speakers wanting me to buy their books. The speakers were not all white and male, and no one asked, "Can I help you?" with the undertone of "You don't belong here."

I had never met a Christian from Korea or sung a song in Malayalam. I didn't know that the majority of the people who followed Jesus were not American or white. I knew about the Underground Railroad but had no idea about China's underground church. This Jesus fascinated me. And standing in the convention hall, where no one was selling anything but instead inviting me to discern what context Jesus was calling me to, I was curious, convicted, and awestruck.

On New Year's Eve at that Urbana, something clicked. I felt it every time I stood in that dome and looked around at the hands raised in praise and adoration. For a few hours, many of the tribes, tongues, and nations that will gather around the throne of God praised him in unison on this side of glory. For a time it was as if all that is promised in Scripture was possible. Maybe there could be reconciliation between the blacks and whites in my town. Perhaps the immigrants who were moving to Southern Virginia didn't have to become black or white to belong and be loved. Though I didn't know where my people were from, perhaps one day Jesus will tell me. In the meantime, life could be joyful amid the suffering and uncertainty. This was not a melting pot where I had to leave behind who I was and fully embrace the dominant monoculture. At Urbana we could bring ourselves to Jesus to mend what had been broken and bring personal, relational, and systemic shalom to the body of Christ.

At that moment I began to seriously question the life, liberty, and the pursuit of everything—except life with Christ. This was the beginning of my discipleship out of WAFR and into the family of God. That is what I truly longed for—not to be a slave, immigrant, or citizen—but the son of a Father who loves me and will do anything for me to know it. That includes descending from heaven to put on flesh and beat death so I know I will beat death too, because he who knew no sin became sin for us that we might become the righteousness of God and abide for eternity with him. He was born, crucified, and raised not that we might become citizens of the United States and call ourselves a city on a hill. There is only one light, Christ. And the true gospel proclaims:

He who believes in Him is not condemned; he who does not believe has been judged already, because he has not believed in the name of the only begotten Son of God. This is the judgment, that the Light has come into the world, and men loved darkness rather than Light, for their deeds were evil. For everyone practicing evil hates the Light, and does not come to the Light for fear that his deeds will be exposed. (John 3:18-20)

To believe, practice, and preach WAFR is to call the darkness light, and the light darkness. Jesus offers his way, his truth, and his life that we might live and be set free. The personal and corporate sins of our individual and collective history, whether committed by us or perpetrated against us, are covered by the blood of Jesus. Thus all people who decide to follow Jesus can lament, confess, repent, and be reconciled to God in Christ by the power of the Holy Spirit.

QUESTIONS FOR INDIVIDUAL REFLECTION AND SMALL GROUP DISCUSSION

- What were your dominant feelings as you read this chapter: curiosity, hope, surprise, confusion, numbness, familiarity, distance, or something else?
- When were those feelings most present?
- What phrases, stories, or historical events resonated with you?
- What events or narratives were you unaware of? What did you learn?
- Where do you disagree or have concerns?
- What questions are you carrying?

GET TO KNOW YOURSELF MORE DEEPLY

- What are your primary feelings toward people of your own ethnic group and heritage?

- What traditions from your family would you want your children to continue?

- What stories, sayings, or songs that shaped your childhood would you want your close friends to know?

- What are two meals that communicate the most about your family or cultural heritage? What is the significance of each dish or unique ingredient?

LIE 4

ALL MEN ARE CREATED EQUAL

WHEN I WAS FIVE I WENT to kindergarten at LaCrosse Elementary School. At first I was in Mrs. Rudd's class. To this day, I remember her being really nice. I spent the days before that Tuesday after Labor Day planning my outfit and asking my older cousins where I was supposed to sit on the bus. My first day of school, I had my cheese sandwich, popcorn, and a nap with snack time afterward. Fighting for Lincoln Logs was my biggest conflict. School was awesome.

But before I got settled, I was switched to Mrs. Lewis's class. She was not Mrs. Rudd but was excited that I was coming to her class. My cheese sandwich, popcorn, and naps with snack time stayed the same. There were Lincoln Logs in this classroom too, but my classmates were different. There were more white students in this room, and this class moved a little faster. I didn't know it then, but my elementary school "tracked" children. "Tracking is the most commonly used term for ability grouping, the practice of lumping children together according to their talents in the classroom."[1] This happened every year, and at first I didn't notice. But in middle and high school it was clear that ability, personality, and sometimes just good behavior separated one group of students from the other. Whether it was Gifted and Talented Education (GATE) in elementary school, the Governor's School Program in high school, or attending Columbia as a Kluge Scholar,[2] we were not all the same. That wasn't something I knew but something I was taught.

If it wasn't clear that each person was created differently in the classroom, then it was loud and clear on the basketball court and the football field. I made the football team in sixth grade and saw the faces of the boys who didn't. I remember what it felt like for the first time to take my shirt off in gym class and compare myself to the boys around me. I remember not being able to dunk. During my junior year, there was a photo in our local paper in which I was racing Eddie Bullock in the 40-yard dash. He probably doesn't remember that photo, but I do because I was behind!

I was left in all of these situations believing one thing and experiencing another. If we are all equal, why can't I dunk or run faster? If we all have the same value and potential, why did I get tracked into a different classroom at every point of my education? Though this perspective may not have been Thomas Jefferson's intention in the Declaration of Independence, it is widely taken to mean an all-encompassing equality, including but not limited to worth, ability, experience, and protection under the law. This is especially true for those who have been or perceive themselves to be disadvantaged. America is where there is supposed to be equal opportunity to pursue life, liberty, and happiness for all people, and that pursuit is protected under the law. Both of these perspectives run away from the gospel and toward idolatry.

More unhelpful, though, is what WAFR would have me believe about my success. According to WAFR, when I succeed it is all *me*. Ultimately, I didn't just work hard, I am actually *better* than those who didn't. Conversely, if we're all equal and I fail, I am to blame and left to wonder what things I need to work on to get what I want by myself. And, ultimately, if I'm not able to attain those things, then other people must be better than me.

SUCCESS AND FAILURE ARE YOUR RESPONSIBILITY

This cycle is destructive but precisely the aim of WAFR. Hard work and effort determine the real value of each person while the veneer of equality is preserved because it sounds good and looks great. "Look what I have! All you need is hard work and dedication" sells more magazines than, "Look at what I have! It's unlikely you'll have as much as me because of how the system works against you, your ethnic group, social class, or gender identity to get to where I am." It makes those at the top of the racial, economic, social, and gender hierarchy feel much better about the inequalities around us that benefit them and stifle others.

We saw this dangerous narrative at play when Hurricane Katrina struck New Orleans (2005) and the destructive earthquake shattered Haiti (2010). After the earthquake, Pat Robertson, a standard bearer of WAFR and chairman of the Christian Broadcasting Network, said, "You know, the Haitians revolted and got themselves free. But ever since, they have been cursed by one thing after the other."[3]

This blaming and shaming doesn't just happen on a large scale but also in everyday suffering. We regularly make the victims responsible for the pain and anguish they experience. It happens to young women on college campuses who are raped at parties when we respond with "She shouldn't have been drinking." It happens every time we see a homeless man on public transit or walking up to our car window. It happens every time a woman is killed in domestic violence and we ask, "Why didn't she leave?" It happens when a thirteen-year-old girl caught in sex trafficking gets blamed because she acted too "grown-up." It is what happened to a deaf man who was killed by police in Oklahoma City. Migdael Sanchez couldn't hear the police telling him to lower the pipe he was holding when they pulled into his yard.[4] Thus, he was shot shortly after and became the 712th person to be killed by police in 2017 in the United States.[5] We ask, *Why was he holding a pipe? Why didn't he put it down? Though he couldn't hear, why didn't he try to communicate?*

Subtly, blame and responsibility are shifted away from the powerful, the bystander, the ignorant, and the indifferent. And those who suffer take the blame and shame that comes from all sides. Since we all are equal, then whatever bad things happen must be our own fault.

The WAFR personal responsibility narrative works the same for those who are exalted by our culture. A single mom, Jelina Sheppard, who went to college despite the difficulties of parenting alone and persevered to graduate, appears on the local five o'clock news. This communicates, "If she can do it, you can too!" [6] The same is true of James Robertson, a poor black man who walked miles to work and then got a free car when someone heard his story.[7] America celebrates their stories, but doesn't ask why Sheppard couldn't get a job that gave her a living wage without a college education or why Robertson wasn't able to afford a car while working full-time at an auto parts plant. No one asks about the income disparity between each of these two and the CEOs of their respective employers. We simply celebrate their hard work and dedication, and proclaim it as evidence of the American dream.

Preserving the image of a society that is polite and respectful and rewards hard work and grit is more important than genuine kindness, justice, and living like every person is made in the image of God.

To reiterate, with the myth that we are all created equal running in the background of the American operating system, adversity turns into a problem for the individual, not for the collective. WAFR's assertion that we are all created equal implies that if I am behind, no one is to blame except me. If equal opportunity is the goal and the reality, then we all have the same starting line. The outcome is my fault or my credit at the end of the day. To implicate the elaborate system of social barriers keeping me, my family, my people group, or my culture in perpetual poverty is a cop-out. I need to take personal responsibility. The effects and influence of barriers and opportunity structures are minimized, if not wholly dismissed.

More pointedly, if I bring up race or gender, at best I just don't understand, or at worst I am manipulative and irresponsible for "playing the race card" or "making it about women." Force, fraud, and coercion should be overcome by my tenacity and determination. Racism, sexism, oppression, and discrimination could not play a role in the pursuit of happiness because we are all created equal.

NOT SO EQUAL

Throughout US history wealthy, connected, white males compose the only group that seems to escape blame and responsibility. Their rights are protected most consistently and often at the expense of other people and the planet. The cases of Robert H. Richards and Ethan Couch illustrate how opportunity bends toward affluent white males.

Richards was found guilty of raping his three-year-old daughter, but because of his connection to the DuPont family and its vast fortune, his legal team was able to mount a defense that spared him spending any time in prison. The judge stated, "The defendant would not fare well in prison," agreeing with Richards's attorneys that an inmate of his status is not a good fit for the penitentiary.

Similarly, Ethan Couch stole beer and took his parents' Ford F-350 out for a ride with seven friends. Tragically, he struck and killed four pedestrians. He pleaded guilty, and at sentencing his lawyers argued that because of his wealth and poor parenting, prison should be out of the question because he couldn't be held responsible for his actions. He was sentenced to rehab and ten years' probation.

Both of these cases argued implicitly that "affluenza" was the culprit, not the individuals themselves. The word *affluenza* was popularized by the 2001 book by the same name. It was used to bolster the argument that their wealth, resources, and position in society caused these men to do such harm. Thus, they should not be punished harshly, if at all. It is safe to assume that if these two men had not been white, wealthy, and defended by well-funded legal teams, their sentences would have been significantly different. For the framers of our nation to say that "all men are created equal" is a lie.

We profess to be kind and value equality and fairness, but the dominant culture encourages pursuing what's better only for *me* and *mine*. Individuals and our collective culture scold our peers and children for believing and acting differently. Here again we have the stark difference between WAFR and genuine Christian faith. WAFR defends hypocrisy and offers weak justifications when called to account, but sincere Christian faith demands confession and repentance.

As I learned in the first foot race I won at five years old and again at the Urbana Missions Conference fifteen years later, none of us are created equal, but all people are made in the image of God. This is the proclamation that brings actual value and validity, inviting us out of WAFR and into the kingdom of God.

The justice of God doesn't treat everyone equally but ascribes indescribable worth, value, and place to each person regardless of race, sexuality, status, or any other box that dominant or marginalized cultures create to elevate or subjugate themselves and others. Followers of Jesus believe that every person is made in God's image and is worthy of the same love, grace, and acceptance that we have been shown. And out of that love and acceptance we work as sons and daughters of the King to restore shalom and forge a more just and reconciled world because God has reconciled us to himself through Christ. And this work is not only because we must maintain our space at his table but also as a loving response to the lavish love that we have been shown.

THE PRODIGAL SON AND THE JUSTICE OF GOD

Jesus' parable of the prodigal son (Luke 15:11-32) shows how the younger son coveted his father's wealth more than he cared for his father's actual life. This becomes clear when the younger son requests his inheritance from his father while he is still alive. To say that this is disrespectful is an understatement. The father, however, responds by giving the requested inheritance. The son, intent on spending this money and enjoying his life apart from his father, goes away and spends all that he has on the pleasures he desired. Upon realizing his terrible decision, the younger son returns home. When he arrives, his father shields him from the stoning that could have been his punishment, celebrates his homecoming, and restores him to the community.

The elder son does not share his father's joy, and thus his desire, though he never left the father, is revealed to be the same as the younger son's. The elder son's desire for his father's wealth is un-earthed in his response to the father's unbridled compassion for the disobedient younger son, who in repentance could risk death by stoning to come home. The elder son, angry and resentful at this cel-ebration, mentions his long-term obedience and devotion to the father. By doing this, the elder son also minimizes the core gift of the father, which is his very presence in the son's life. The sons in this story illustrate what many people in America desire and what the god of America promises—to give us life, liberty, and whatever else we want that will make us happy, comfortable, and secure. This is juxta-posed with the God of Abraham, Isaac, and Jacob, who desires to give us himself through Christ by the power of the Holy Spirit, which will yield eternal satisfaction.

HOW GOD HONORS THOSE IN THE BODY OF CHRIST

The distinction between WAFR and biblical Christianity is further developed in 1 Corinthians 12:12-27. Here the apostle Paul says the justice of God not only ascribes value but balances the scales by favoring the weak, powerless, and vulnerable. Paul says the one body of Christ (the church) has many members. All parts of the body—and consequently all people in creation—are necessary for the flourishing of the body of Christ. The passage in context though goes even further. Specifically, verses 21-27 say,

> The eye cannot say to the hand, "I have no need of you"; or again the head to the feet, "I have no need of you." On the contrary, it is much truer that the members of the body which seem to be weaker are necessary; and those *members* of the body which we deem less honorable, on these we bestow more abundant honor, and our less presentable members become much more pre-sentable, whereas our more presentable members have no need *of it*. But God has *so* composed the body, giving more abundant honor to that *member* which lacked, so that there may be no division in the body, but *that* the members may have the same

care for one another. And if one member suffers, all the members suffer with it; if *one* member is honored, all the members rejoice with it.

WAFR would not dispute the ideas in this passage. Yet its intention and impact have been vigorously resisted in America—especially in "Christian" contexts. Obviously, an eye and a finger do not have the same function. Paul is pressing for fairness, not sameness. This imagery applies today as immigrant American churches, female theologians, and voices not aligned with the power structures of WAFR are quieted or left out altogether. No more acutely is this reality felt than in moments of social trauma.

WHO GETS TO BE HONORED?

After seeing Terence Crutcher murdered by a police officer in Tulsa, Oklahoma, I couldn't stop crying.[8] I wept in a church service because though I was inside a church with white Christians, I was somehow outside of this body of Christ. There had been no mention of this incident or the hundreds of other police shootings that claimed the lives of men and women who shared my skin color and possibly our faith. Furthermore, after reading Franklin Graham's latest message telling me to "Listen up! Do what the police say," among other ignorant, uninformed, racialized statements, I literally had to go and lie down.[9] His post made the words to Dara Maclean's "Blameless" and many contemporary Christian worship songs feel out of reach for the black boy inside of me that once again would be seen as a threat to be put down, not a son to be picked up. More accurately, the chorus would be,

> Blameless,
> You call *them* Holy.
> *They've* been forgiven
> You call *them* righteous *they are yours*.
> *They're* spotless

You call *them* worthy
They are Your children
You call *them* chosen.
They're yours.[10]

"Them" being white people. White people are blameless, holy, forgiven, righteous, and belong to God. White people are spotless, worthy, chosen, and children of God—not we whose skin is kissed by the sun, whose eyes are almond shaped, or would dare claim a tribe or native name.

I associate being theologically accurate with white people.[11] I associate being well-thought-out with being white. I associate being trustworthy and good with being white. Everything biblically sound about Christianity that is produced by nonwhite people must be approved by white people at white seminaries. Spirituals with four lines said over and over must not be as holy as hymns with four stanzas. Being at church for four hours is inefficient, and a good sermon has three points. And the only worship song that gets introduced as *new*, *different*, and *something we are trying* is a gospel song played once a year. There is an inferiority that I and other nonwhite people are fed and have internalized, and it robs us of joy, peace, and love. We take the back seat, or get off the bus altogether, because WAFR is a theological Jim Crow in which the cross is changed from a lynching tree for an impoverished Jew to a lunch counter in 1950s Greensboro.[12] *This* is not good news at all to African Americans. The lightweight promise of white evangelicalism is crushed by the real lives of people of color.

American, *Christian*, *white*, and *male* are disturbingly synonymous terms. What is most familiar to me in prayer and worship isn't just unfamiliar to white American Christians, it's "unbiblical." It's so different that it can't be Christian. To weep and wail at the front of the church, to call for reconciliation from the pulpit, and to pray for hours in tongues with no interpreter present is not foreign to me. These feel more than appropriate to me because my brothers and sisters of color are being murdered by police who "fear" for their lives, and my "Christian brothers and sisters" are too busy defending themselves to make space for us and our pain. In WAFR there is no room for pain, grief, and loss.

Into this reality drop these words of Paul: we who are feared, marginalized, and oppressed are *indispensable* and will receive *honor*. Paul goes on to say,

> God has *so* composed the body, giving more abundant honor to that *member* which lacked, so that there may be no division in the body, but *that* the members may have the same care for one another. And if one member suffers, all the members suffer with it; if *one* member is honored, all the members rejoice with it. (1 Corinthians 12:24-26)

So when I say that my black life matters, I am not minimizing or denigrating my brother or sister who does not hold the same racial assignment. Instead, they can stand beside me with lighter skin and say the same thing, because both of us are made in the image of God. And in this kingdom, we can suffer, mourn, and weep together. Moreover, we can rejoice in the hope of Christ without minimizing the grief, fear, and present danger. The two, lament and joy, can exist in the same space, at peace with one another.

The second verse of "Blameless" is so powerful because of this truth.

I will boldly come
Running straight to the One
Singing over me
Your songs of salvation
No one can take this from me
I am a child that You name free
Nothing will separate us
I'm held by You.

This is the reward of God. His presence is with us for all eternity. It is not his stuff but God himself that is offered. In the face of deputies who are intimidated because I wear a Colin Kaepernick jersey and say "black lives matter," I am a child that God named "free." In the presence of folks uncomfortable with my worship, I can raise my hands and shout aloud because no one can take away the joy that my Father has given me. I need not be ashamed.

No matter how strong the prison-industrial complex is or how heavy of a burden history and the media place on my black back, nothing will separate me from my Father in heaven because I am covered by the blood of Christ Jesus.

NO FAVORITISM

It doesn't matter how segregated our worship may be on Sunday mornings, the kingdom of God has enough room in the program for our praise and our pain. The altar is big enough for all of us who cry, and the aisles are wide enough for us all to run and dance. Franklin Graham may not see me, but my Father in heaven surely does, and the day will come when every tribe and every tongue and every nation will praise and worship him in the heavenly places. And confessing that you are a white American evangelical is *not* the price of admission to the kingdom. In fact, to center racial, national, and folk religious identity over Jesus will lead to eternal damnation.

God shows no favoritism to the rich, connected, and those of earthly power and influence. Jesus' brother explains this in James 2:1-13, and the Acts church put it into practice. God reengineered the social fabric of the early church in Acts 6 when the Hebraic Jews discriminated against the Hellenistic Jewish widows in the daily distribution of food. Instead of correcting this problem by giving 50 percent of the power to the marginalized and 50 percent to the Hebrews, he gave all power and responsibility for distribution to the marginalized group. This would be like allowing African Americans to have total access and leadership over education in America, or Native Americans taking over the Departments of Agriculture, Interior, Transportation, State, Defense, and Homeland Security—putting them in charge over the system that exploited them and then submitting to their leadership.

This happened in Scripture when we see Stephen, a Greek Jew, preaching the gospel of Christ after having been selected by early church leaders to take over the distribution of food. Stephen was lower class and lower status, but not according to the kingdom of God. He was wise, full of the spirit and wisdom, and therefore qualified and worthy of leadership.

In an unjust society, we are not seen and do not live as equals. But God created us all with equal worth and value, and we all have equal access to God in Christ. In a fallen world we are not created equal and thus don't have equal opportunity to succeed in the race for life, liberty, and the pursuit of happiness. In present-day America, to take the Constitution and extrapolate equal value for every person is like putting a brand-new paint job, tinted windows, and fresh tires on a car with no engine or seats. It looks great on the outside but was never meant to move forward or carry anyone.

The framers of the US government only included white, land-owning men of good social standing as enfranchised citizens. They did not believe that *all* humans were created equal and therefore had no intention of entitling all people to equal treatment. They also took steps to ensure that people outside of their circles wouldn't receive equal treatment. In 1787, James Madison said in the "Secret Proceedings of the Constitutional Debates of the Convention" that the Senate "ought to be so constituted as to protect the minority of the opulent against the majority."[13]

But if we revise history to create a corporate narrative that we are a Christian nation of immigrants seeking better lives, we can dictate what the individual value and identity of each person are as well. The Declaration of Independence's statement that "We hold these truths to be self-evident that all men are created equal" is perplexing at best and at worst a declaration that all who are not male, white, and wealthy are not equal and are presumably less than those gathered together in 1787. This country's actual history and lived reality reveals that this declaration of equality is the opposite of what was actually intended by its authors and experienced by natives, women, and minorities.

Without being rooted in a practical theology that values the truth that all people are made in the image of an objective, all-knowing, and loving God, this statement is an impeccable brochure for a land that doesn't exist. In reality, whole swaths of God's creation are left on the outside of those supposed all-inclusive statements. In biblical Christianity, God alone confers value and identity—not presidents, senators, or representatives.

When the idol of America isn't central but the resurrected Christ is, profound transformation is not just possible but inevitable. And not just in Scripture but in our present day.

RESISTING THE VIOLENCE OF INEQUALITY

In July 2016, the results of normalized violence and devaluing of human beings were on full display thanks to cell phone cameras and social media. Philando Castile was murdered in front of his wife and child, and Alton Sterling was shot and killed by police while being held face down.[14] Not only that, Micah Xavier Johnson shot and killed five police officers in Dallas, no doubt in response to the more than three hundred police-involved killings of African American men and women in that past year.[15] It was a watershed moment for many inside and outside the African American community. Police brutality is neither new nor infrequent. It is as normal and prevalent as getting up in the morning, drinking coffee, and going to bed at night. Though these realities may be felt acutely in communities of color, white Americans are not immune and suffer tragedies under militarized policing as well, though they too don't hold headlines for long.[16]

Injustices like this are not just anomalies or outliers, but intentional, extended, well-documented patterns of thought, behavior, and systems that normalize pain and suffering for large groups of people. That week in July led UN Human Rights expert Ricardo A. Sunga III, the chair of the United Nations panel, to say, "The killings also demonstrate a high level of structural and institutional racism. The United States is far from recognizing the same rights for all its citizens. Existing measures to address racist crimes motivated by prejudice are insufficient and have failed to stop the killings."[17]

Although these systems of brokenness may change appearance, their premise remains firmly intact. Systemic oppression in the criminal justice system gives empirical evidence that sin and evil exist in this world. The documentary *13th* by Ava DuVernay, *The New Jim Crow* by Michelle Alexander, and *Just Mercy* by Bryan Stevenson are three recent resources that connect the dots of racism, sexism, and oppression from 1619 to today.

Had I been alone, the weight of July 2016 would have crushed me as an African American male in the United States, but I had a diverse community of committed followers of Jesus to lament, confess, repent, and pursue shalom with me. Sophia Gaboury, a formerly undocumented Filipina college graduate in New York City now serving as NYC area director for InterVarsity Christian Fellowship, was the leader of the team I served with. She was willing to change the schedule of our meeting and center on the work of Jesus, not the work we had on our to-do lists. Our agenda changed to make space for the grief and fear in the room as well as the ignorance and confusion that police brutality and violence brings to the surface. Our team of men and women, with backgrounds from India, Guatemala, Haiti, Scotland, Ireland, Germany, Hawaii, and Japan, lamented, confessed, and looked to Jesus, walking with him into our pain, fear, confusion, and questions—together.

Additionally, two InterVarsity leaders, Jason Gaboury and Carolyn Carney (both seen as white in this country), regularly press into the tensions to center on Jesus and normalize the experiences of staff, students, and the wider communities of color. They intentionally create space for people under their leadership not just to fit in but to belong, take up space, and lead. These three people of God, and the diverse teams I have the privilege of knowing and serving alongside, till the soil of my heart to grow seeds of peace where there is so much pain and strife.

Because of leaders like this, I believe it is possible, in moments of great pain where sin and evil are so apparent, to turn away from the idol of WAFR and see one another as people made in the image of God, worthy of love, grace, and truth, and praise Jesus. When I am with them, I am reminded that we are not hamsters on wheels of prosperity. We are sons and daughters of the Most High God, saved by grace, and set free to heal as we've been healed.

QUESTIONS FOR INDIVIDUAL REFLECTION AND SMALL GROUP DISCUSSION

- What were your dominant feelings as you read this chapter: curiosity, hope, surprise, confusion, numbness, familiarity, distance, or something else?

- When were those feelings most present?

- What phrases, stories, or historical events resonated with you?

- What events or narratives were you unaware of? What did you learn?

- Where do you disagree or have concerns?

- What questions are you carrying?

MAKING JESUS BIGGER THAN SUFFERING AND INJUSTICE

What issues or problems do you feel are overwhelming and make it difficult to see God and his people working to change? Perhaps it's sexual assault, police brutality, abortion, divorce, or addiction in your own family. Make a list and write down whatever comes to mind.

With that issue in mind, please turn to appendix 3. Lament, confession, repentance, and reconciliation are four steps in responding to suffering and seeking justice with Christ at the center.

LIE 5

WE ARE A GREAT DEMOCRACY

THE FIRST TIME I PAID ATTENTION to a presidential election was 2000. I was a freshman in high school in South Hill, Virginia, and our schoolwide mock election between George Bush and Al Gore was very close. Virginia may not have been known as a swing state in that year, but my school certainly was. Later that evening and in the days to come, I was confused about how Al Gore could win the majority of votes but still lose the election. Fortunately, in Virginia, civics education is still a part of our regular education. This was a real-time education on the Electoral College.

Alexander Hamilton, James Madison, and others saw a republic as the best form of government, saying it was fair and necessary to prevent anarchy, dictatorship, and . . . democracy. The Constitution and its supporting documents thus cast a vision for a republic where power is held by voters *and* their elected representatives. Contrary to that narrative, the majority of Americans assert that the United States is the greatest democracy in the world.

Democracy comes from two Greek words: *demos*, meaning "people," and *kratos*, meaning "power." Literally, it could mean "power to the people" or "majority rule." *Republic*, on the other hand, comes from two Latin words, *res*, meaning "thing," and *publica*, meaning "public." This can and is often extrapolated to mean that America is a people of public things, and those public things are *laws*. These laws are a set of common rules that govern society and set the precedent for police forces, the criminal justice system, and so on. Therefore, because the United States claims to be a nation of laws implemented by democratically elected officials, it identifies itself as a democratic republic. The fact that America functions as a republic and not a democracy shouldn't come as a surprise to US citizens, but it does. This is most evident every time a presidential candidate wins the Electoral College but loses the popular vote. If America was a true democracy, that would not be possible.

This truth surprises US citizens because we are generally uninformed about historical and current events, world affairs, and the implications of basic policy proposals at every level of government. A study by the Center for Information and Research on Civic Learning and Engagement at Tufts University found the following:

- Most states do not emphasize civic education, which includes learning about citizenship, government, law, current events, and related topics.

- In 2012, only twenty-one states required a state-designed social studies test—a significant decrease from 2001, when thirty-four states conducted regular assessments on social studies subjects.

- Only nine states require students to pass a social studies test to graduate from high school: Alabama, Georgia, Mississippi, New Mexico, New York, Ohio, South Carolina, Texas, and Virginia.

- Only eight states administer statewide, standardized tests specifically in civics/American government: California, Indiana, Kansas, Kentucky, Missouri, Ohio, Virginia, and West Virginia. Only Ohio and Virginia require students to pass the test to graduate.

This lack of knowledge about the political process is not limited to the poor or those living in rural areas, as evidenced by presidential candidate and former two-time governor of New Mexico Gary Johnson, who, during a line of questioning about foreign affairs did not know where or what Aleppo was.[1] To the shock of the interviewer, he genuinely had no idea. But when told that it was in Syria, he gave an opinion on this entrenched geopolitical conflict even though he had

admitted ignorance on a conflict that afflicts millions of people.[2] Gary
Johnson is not an anomaly but the norm.

To put it concisely, the US Constitution, Declaration of Independence, *Federalist Papers*, and state constitutions don't include the word *democracy*. In fact, those who gathered for the Constitutional Convention in 1787 were heavily invested in creating a stable system of government that maintained the best lives for themselves and those they cared about—male, white, and wealthy.

In *Federalist Papers* 10, James Madison said,

> Democracies have ever been spectacles of turbulence and contention; have ever been found incompatible with personal security or the rights of property; and have in general been as short in their lives as they have been violent in their deaths— Theoretic politicians, who have patronized this species of government, have erroneously supposed that by reducing mankind to a perfect equality in their political rights, they would at the same time be perfectly equalized and assimilated in their possessions, their opinions, and their passions.[3]

Alexander Hamilton took it a step further to hone in on the fear of an uninformed, easily swayed population: "We are a republican government. Real liberty isn't found in despotism or the extremes of democracy but in moderate governments."[4]

And John Adams did not hold back in his critique of democracy:

> Democracy has never been and never can be so durable as aristocracy or monarchy; but while it lasts, it is more bloody than either. . . . Remember, democracy never lasts long. It soon wastes, exhausts, and murders itself. There never was a democracy yet that did not commit suicide. It is in vain to say that democracy is less vain, less proud, less selfish, less ambitious, or less avaricious than aristocracy or monarchy. It is not true, in fact, and nowhere appears in history. Those passions are the same in all men, under all forms of simple government, and

when unchecked, produce the same effects of fraud, violence, and cruelty. When clear prospects are opened before vanity, pride, avarice, or ambition, for their easy gratification, it is hard for the most considerate philosophers and the most conscientious moralists to resist the temptation.[5]

FALSE EMPOWERMENT

Though I read quotes like those above in my history classes, it is still jarring to dwell on the reality that the United States is not a democracy and that democracy was not what the forefathers actually intended. I believe the source of that surprise is my desire to both feel and be a part of something bigger than myself. I also believe this is the attractive but false empowerment that characterizes white American folk religion. To propagate the myth of direct democracy in America creates a false perception of meaningful involvement and exaggerates a citizen's influence. Moreover, a republic set up to protect the rich and powerful while presenting itself as a direct democracy is a lie to keep people like me running the race for life, liberty, and happiness.

On its face, WAFR is empowering to everybody willing to get on the race track. It would be great to think that I, an African American male, might have the opportunity to forgo the tragedy-laden history of my people and worship a god that wants me to work hard for the best life and pursue happiness because I have the choice to do so. It is tempting to embrace the immigrant narrative and take my place in the "melting pot" to contribute all I can. And to be told that America is a democracy means that not only can I work but I also have access to power.

As civil rights leader John Lewis advocates and the movie *Selma* captures so brilliantly, the vote gives African Americans and other groups access to power. But I contend that it only gives the *illusion* of access to power and is a consistently underwhelming invitation to influence. I used to believe that democracy meant there is the potential for power structures to change, and voting was the way to do it. I thought voting meant that my voice and perspective mattered and that my efforts to engage would be taken seriously by those seeking my support. Voting was value and validation.

The level of trust I had in our government, my citizenship, and my ability to vote now feels naive, shallow, and idealistic, but that is how WAFR works. Without critical thinking and reflection, I committed myself to catch phrases, slogans, and emotional whims while dismissing history and evidence-based research. If, as Hebrews 11:1 says, "Faith is the substance of things hoped for and evidence of things unseen" (KJV), then faith is required to put my hope and trust in this country. Many communities of color have never seen this country's promises made manifest, yet we are to put trust and confidence in it without question or protest. This expectation of un-wavering hope and trust connected to a set of actions such as pledging allegiance, standing for an anthem, and honoring politicians and military personnel regardless of their integrity sounds less like a country and more like a religion.

The notion of "pressing forward to become all I can be" is the belief that once I get there, life will be amazing and all that I dreamed of. We see this in the latest commercials for new cars and gadgets. Advertise-ments claim these products are the answers to every problem. Yet once we have them, others are already in production and are said to be better than what we now have.

My personal experience tells a story where hard work, raw talent, and passion are rewarded. But research and my relationships tell a different narrative. The fact that I have a different personal experience doesn't mean that the systemic reality isn't true. Voter suppression, lobbying, campaign finance reform, gerrymandering, and voter turnout are four levers that keep the republic in place, maintaining the status quo that the US founding fathers sought to protect. Most important though is that this entire system, like every political system, is at odds with God the Father seated on the throne in glory with Jesus at his right hand.

LEVER 1: VOTER SUPPRESSION

According to *The 21st-Century Voter*, voter suppression

> refers to legislative and nonlegislative actions designed to discourage—if not prevent—a segment of voters from casting ballots during elections in hopes of affecting election outcomes. Voter suppression activities range from restrictive policies that make the voting process inconvenient or impossible for some voters, to efforts designed to spread misinformation about campaigns or voting procedures, to outright psychological and physical intimidation.[6]

As we saw in chapter one, voter suppression can be embedded in the law as these three cases show:

- 1790: The United States did not have a national policy for voting until 1790.[7] The Naturalization Law states that "free White men of good standing" could vote. Prior to that, only white men who owned property (including owning women and slaves) over twenty-one years old were eligible to vote in most states. Therefore, Native Americans, slaves, free blacks, women, indentured servants, the poor, and immigrants from Asia and Latin America were outside of the political process.

- 1887: The Dawes Act made it possible for Native Americans to vote if they gave up their tribal affiliation.

- 1792 to the present: Since 1792, the United States has allowed varying levels of voter disenfranchisement based on felony convictions. Many of these laws were an effort to keep communities of color away from the ballot box, especially when the thirteenth and fourteenth amendments were passed during Reconstruction in the South after the Civil War.

The most aggressive, egregious, and well-known forms of voter suppression occurred in the Jim Crow era of the post-Civil War South. "The segregation and disenfranchisement laws known as 'Jim Crow'

represented a formal, codified system of racial apartheid that dominated the American South for three quarters of a century beginning
in the 1890's."[8] This terrible and well-documented system undergirded
the context for poll taxes, complex voter ID laws, and voting tests that
kept African Americans and poor whites out of the voting process.
Additionally, violent mobs, not just the KKK, made sure these laws
were enforced, and those who challenged this social order were intimidated, injured, or killed. The "Ballad of Harry Moore" by poet
Langston Hughes, later put to melody by Sweet Honey in the Rock,
tells the story of the Florida NAACP leader who registered many black
Americans to vote.[9] In retaliation, his home was bombed by the KKK
on Christmas night 1951. He died on the way to the hospital, and his
wife passed away nine days later, leaving behind two young daughters.

In this poem there is a horrid picture of suffering and pain where
the struggle for change meets militarized racism. To imagine so vividly
the silent promise of Christmas night shattered by the sound of
exploding hatred is beyond language. I could press into hopefulness if
actions like these were confined to the history books. But in North
Carolina, Texas, and states around the country, cases of discriminatory voter ID laws and voter intimidation by neo-Nazis and hate
groups in urban polling places. Right now, those who advocate for
equal voting rights are threatened with violence, rape, and murder.[10]

In 2016, I learned of the work that the Reverend William Barber
and many others did to challenge voter suppression laws that
targeted "black and African American communities with almost
surgical precision" in North Carolina.[11] Barber's situation is not an
outlier or a special case. Texas, Indiana, Wisconsin, Florida, and
other states have also passed laws and changed voting processes
that disproportionately affected minority, urban, or impoverished
communities, and came under legal challenge. For example, in
many states African Americans have to wait twice as long as white
citizens at voting polls. In 2012, this was said to have turned
730,000 people away from the polls. Additionally, purging names

from registration lists disproportionately affects communities of color. Under this practice in Florida, 87 percent of those names brought into question were minorities.[12]

We are taken aback by stories like this if they make it through our social media filters. We are briefly challenged by the reality of voter suppression in the United States. We might exclaim, "How can this *still* be happening?" and then turn the page in the newspaper or retweet quickly before scrolling down to the next story on our Twitter feed. But if we engage fully for longer than a minute, discomfort sets in when we ponder that the democracy we purport does not function as we believe.

LEVER 2: GERRYMANDERING

Gerrymandering is the drawing of political boundaries to give one political party a numeric advantage over an opposing party.[13] It could also be called "redistricting," but it is different in that it explicitly gives one political party or candidate a blatant advantage over another. Usually, it favors those with power and resources, and gives them the best chance to keep the power and resources they possess. This type of political gaming is older than the United States. Before the Constitution was ratified, Virginia governor Patrick Henry asked for the fifth district to be redrawn in order to make the path to victory easier for one of his political allies. The term itself comes from Eldridge Gerry, governor of Massachusetts in 1812. An article featured a picture of a salamander, because that most closely resembled the shape of the district that Governor Gerry created. Thus the term *gerrymandering* was born and lives on to this day.[14]

States such as Wisconsin, North Carolina, and Texas have cases to be argued in front of the Supreme Court with significant implications for the practice going forward. In the majority of cases, elected officials and party leaders actually draw the district lines themselves to ensure victory, and there exists no legal penalty for doing so. The only illegality exists when the lines are drawn specifically on racial/ethnic boundaries. The two most common forms of gerrymandering are called "packing" and "cracking." Packing occurs when one cultural group is drawn into a district, and cracking happens when a certain group is intentionally spread to minimize their impact. Both of these strategies are meant to minimize the influence of that demographic and ensure victory for the party in charge. Both political parties in America participate in this practice.

It is well-known that these districts are drawn along racial, ethnic, and socioeconomic lines to disenfranchise voters in both parties, but since politicians claim that the districts are drawn along party lines, it is not against the law. North Carolina State Representative David Lewis made this point plain, as he explained in 2016 after North Carolina state maps were deemed unconstitutional because of racial discrimination: "We want to make clear that . . . to the extent [we] are going to use political data in drawing this map, it is to gain partisan advantage on the map. I want that criteria to be clearly stated and understood."[15]

It is clear that the idol of power reigns with little resistance. Each side waits not merely for the chance to make a just case to voters but to win and have the opportunity to manipulate the maps so as to hold on to political influence. As Jeremy Mayer of George Mason University bluntly remarked, "It is not the case of voters choosing their politicians but politicians choosing their voters."[16] And with how the US government functions in the present day, gerrymandering looks like it will continue in perpetuity, segregating districts in ways that suit the powerful and further disenfranchise the powerless.

What the Republican Party was aiming for in 2016 worked in North Carolina. Republicans only received 53 percent of the votes, but they won 77 percent of the seats in the state legislature. The Republicans invested thirty million dollars in the REDMAP or the Redistricting Majority Project. Nationwide in 2012, Democratic candidates received over one million votes more than Republicans, but Republicans sent thirty-three more of their candidates to the House of Representatives. Democrats are not innocent, and states such as New York, Maryland,

and Illinois are guilty of radical partisan divisions that refocus power and control as well.[17] For example, Democrat Hakeem Jefferies ran against a fellow Democratic incumbent for the New York State Assembly seat and lost 59 percent to 41 percent.[18] Two years later, the district was redrawn to carve Jeffries's residence out of the 57th District altogether. Thus, his supporters who expected to see his name on the ballot found that they no longer resided in the district they had lived in for decades.

Even if citizens have the right to vote, the goal of the forefathers is at work to prevent a truly democratic society, one where the majority rules. This is not the way power works in the kingdom of God. Yet it is the way of WAFR, which claims democracy and empowerment for all people on the one hand while ensuring that power is concentrated and highly controlled on the other.

LEVER 3: LOBBYING AND CAMPAIGN FINANCE REFORM

The role of money in politics adds to this troubling pattern of intentional exclusion. Two aspects in particular are problematic: lobbying and campaign finance.

Lobbying is "the act of attempting to influence the actions, policies, or decisions of officials in their daily life, most often legislators or leaders of regulatory agencies."[19] Campaign finance refers to all funds raised to promote candidates, political parties, or policy initiatives. Political parties, charitable organizations, and political action committees (PACs) are vehicles used in aggregating funds to keep campaigns alive. After the landmark case *Citizens United v. FEC*, decided by the Supreme Court in 2010, money flooded into America's political processes at an unprecedented rate.

Citizens United created the context where corporations were recognized as individuals, which unleashed unlimited corporate funds into the political process in the United States. Citizens United, a nonprofit organization, asserted that if a corporation is recognized as an individual, then it has First Amendment protections like speech.

Except in this case, corporate money is that speech. Citizens United pushed against the Federal Election Commission and the 1971 law that created it. Under the Federal Election Campaign Act, there were strict limits on the amount of money that an individual, corporation, or group could donate to a political candidate. Additionally, candidates had to disclose who their campaign contributions came from. The McCain-Feingold Act and other laws sought to limit the influence of money in politics as well.

The controversy arose in 2008 because Citizens United spent over one million dollars on a documentary criticizing Hillary Clinton in her primary race against Barack Obama.[20] Her campaign sued to prevent the release of the documentary because it could be seen as "electioneering communication" or material attempting to sway voters. Citizens United argued that to not show the documentary infringed on their right to free speech. Ultimately, this landmark case went to the US Supreme Court, and the court sided with Citizens United, thus making it legal for corporations, unions, individuals, and other groups to give unlimited sums of money to support or oppose political candidates. Since then, the costs of campaigns have skyrocketed, with the Barack Obama versus Mitt Romney race in 2012 costing nearly a combined $2 billion dollars.[21] Only eight years later, Hillary Clinton and Donald Trump would combine to spend $2.4 billion on their campaigns.[22]

Similarly, corporations and special interest groups also vied for power and influence. Lobbying was a four billion dollar industry in 2017 with one billion dollars alone being spent in the first quarter of 2017.[23] Lobbyists do everything from talking with politicians to drafting fill-in-the-blank bills for representatives and senators. A short, straight line of people ties together corporations, lobbyists, government officials, lucrative contracts, and policies to benefit all those involved. For example, Florida lobbyist and super PAC leader Brian Ballard earned more than one million dollars within a three-month period after the 2016 election. His firm, Ballard Partners, along with a dozen other lobbying groups with close ties to Trump, signed deals with foreign governments and multinational corporations at a staggering pace in an attempt to influence the White House and wider US policy. Ballard's firm received payments from the Dominican Republic, the Socialist Party of Albania, and GEO Group, which won bids to build immigrant prisons that no doubt affect the United States' policies on immigration. The White House responded that President Trump had a

> great number of highly talented people working on his campaign. It isn't a surprise those who did not choose to join the adminis-tration are highly successful in whatever endeavor they undertake. There is no legal restriction from former campaign aides having positive relationships inside and outside the White House.[24]

Relationships among the wealthy and connected benefit the wealthy and connected, while refugees, migrants, the undocumented, the poor, and those lacking connections to these exclusive networks hold no sway or influence because they cannot compete with the vast financial resources and personnel of these interest groups. In this structure, faithfully executing Proverbs 31:8-9 is impossible.

> Open your mouth for the mute,
> For the rights of all the unfortunate.
> Open your mouth, judge righteously,
> And defend the rights of the afflicted and needy.

Popularly translated it says, "Be a voice for the voiceless." But in America, money and wealth literally speak on behalf of those who have money and wealth, and against those who lack it.

LEVER 4: VOTER TURNOUT

The efforts to suppress voter turnout, gerrymander districts, and allow an unlimited amount of corporate money to influence elections lead to the belief that voting doesn't matter. This might explain why 28 percent of eligible voters turned out for the 2016 presidential primary, and in the 2016 presidential election, only 61 percent of eli-gible voters, or 137 million people, cast their ballots.[25]

Compared to other developed countries, the United States ranks very low in turnout. According to the Daily Dot,

> Americans are one of the least active voting populations among developed countries, with the U.S. clocking in at 31 out of 35 countries in voter turnout. Take Belgium, which saw over 87% of voters' turnout in 2014, or Denmark, where 80% percent of voters made it out to the polls.[26]

In Belgium, it is against the law not to vote. And in Denmark, voters don't have to register; it is done automatically. In both countries, the election season is short, focus on issues is high, and diverse demographics trust the election process. These are not the norms in America.

The breakdown of the data shows that the majority of white men and women with higher education and access to resources dominate the voting population in the United States. Minority populations can tip political contests, but the interests of minorities cannot compete with corporations and special interests that fund campaigns. Democracy simply isn't possible when a country is not hearing from 70 percent of the population, which comprise the poor, isolated, and underresourced from all races in every corner of the country.

Though those on both sides of the aisle and of differing political stripes may say the system needs fixing and can't be trusted, we must understand that the system is working as designed. America's founding documents (for example, the Declaration of Independence and the Constitution) reflect political processes that are working as they should be. The words of our forefathers, who founded WAFR, ensured that the United States functions the way it does. Are meetings of white men with means who write laws today truly any different than those who gathered for constitutional conventions that founded this nation?[27] Moreover, when CEOs make more than three hundred times the average employee, women of color make 69 cents to the dollar of white men, the top 0.1 percent of Americans control more wealth than the bottom 90 percent, and at least eighty million people don't vote, it is clear that the system is changing to keep conditions the same, not to benefit those continually disenfranchised.[28] Yet the persistent narrative that things are getting better is exactly what many preach and believe.

HYPOCRISY VERSUS INTEGRITY

WAFR has no problem with movements such as "Rock the Vote," knowing money in politics and gerrymandering dictate who wins the election and lobbyists write the laws. And, consistent with the views of James Madison, Alexander Hamilton, and John Adams, it is perfectly acceptable for power to be held in the hands of a few at the expense of all others.

The message of Jesus Christ is contrary to this reality. He is the Prince of Peace seated at the right hand of God. Like the United States, the kingdom of God is not a democracy but something altogether different. It's not a democracy; we did not elect our King. But it is not a typical monarchy or theocracy because this King enters into the messiness of the fight for power, influence, and resources as God incarnate in Christ Jesus. Not the thin-lipped, light-skinned, flowing-hair Jesus—but the brown-skinned Christ who suffered under both Roman empirical oppression and the Pharisees' abusive religious power. God's plan was never to set up a nation-state with rules, laws, and a military. His rule makes order out of chaos, and as Father and God, he ensures the flourishing of all creation through establishing his kingdom.

Some historians point out that when the tragic political truth emerges and disenfranchised people rise up and resist, they look for a leader and long for liberation. This is true of every human in history, which is why the message of Jesus speaks to all generations and is eternally relevant. For Christians, the Savior has come and his name is Jesus.

But since WAFR has redefined what it means to be a Christian, this is not the Christ that many have met. WAFR casts a vision for individuals and the nation that sets the stage for the grand illusion of input, inclusion, and self-importance. The Jesus of Scripture enters here.

Those desiring to follow Jesus don't get to vote on his platform or give input on his policies. We petition through prayer and supplication with thanksgiving, desiring to be in accordance with his will at all times, regardless of the political structures we find ourselves in. True disciples must practice an authentic public faith that prioritizes the things of God without compromising to control people or attain power. We are called to radical servant leadership in submission to God's order of personal, relational, and systemic shalom. This is true regardless of the political power structure at work because Jesus' kingdom is not of this world and God is sovereign.

This made no sense to Peter as he rebuked Jesus for proclaiming that he would suffer and be crucified. Matthew 16:21-23 reads (with my additions):

> From that time on Jesus began to show His disciples [clearly] that He must go to Jerusalem, and suffer many things from the elders and the chief priests and scribes [the Sanhedrin, Jewish high court], and be killed, and be raised up [from death to life] on the third day. Peter took Him aside and began to rebuke Him, saying, "God forbid it, Lord! This will never happen to You." But Jesus turned and said to Peter, "Get behind Me, Satan! You are a stumbling block to Me; for you are not setting your mind on God's interest, but man's."

It seems that Peter didn't receive the message, because he lashed out in violence during Jesus' arrest as we observe vividly in John 18:10-11: "Simon Peter then, having a sword, drew it and struck the high priest's slave, and cut off his right ear; and the slave's name was Malchus. So Jesus said to Peter, 'Put the sword into the sheath; the cup which the Father has given Me, shall I not drink it?'"

It made no sense to an oppressed, marginalized people to not get a say and to have no input in this plan for freedom and salvation. It made even less sense to have their leader suffer shame, humiliation, violence, and death. This was not a "win" for the Israelites against the violent oppression of the Romans; it was another humiliating loss. Similarly, I am confounded by a Jesus that doesn't form a posse, collect weapons, and fight back. Yet when I actually reflect on the grace, peace, and salvation available to me and all people in the past, present, and future, I am deeply grateful that democracy is not the way of Christ.

Jesus' actions here are consistent with the system of rule that he, the Father, and the Holy Spirit intend. Its values of mercy, justice, love, and judgment are at work no matter what political system his followers find themselves in. Our task as his children, then, is as it has been since the Great Commission was first given—to ask God how can we bear witness within whatever political system we find ourselves while not grasping for or idolizing the earthly power, influence, and resources we possess. Instead, we are to leverage them all for his glory and the flourishing of all, especially the poor, marginalized, and oppressed, in loving obedience to God, who loved us first.

QUESTIONS FOR INDIVIDUAL REFLECTION AND SMALL GROUP DISCUSSION

- What were your dominant feelings as you read this chapter: curiosity, hope, surprise, confusion, numbness, familiarity, distance, or something else?
- When were those feelings most present?
- What phrases, stories, or historical events resonated with you?
- What events or narratives were you unaware of? What did you learn?
- Where do you disagree or have concerns?
- What questions are you carrying?

EXPLORE YOUR POLITICAL ICEBERG

Many of our core beliefs about politics come from experiences we have had, the communities we come from, and the families we grew up in. Our engagement with systems and structures isn't usually informed by mature, individual, and corporate encounters with God in Scripture. With at least two friends, one being from a background similar to yours and another who may disagree with you on issues like abortion, the death penalty, climate legislation, military spending, and health care, discuss the following questions:

- What is the role of faith in politics?

- What does your family or faith community believe the role of faith is outside of personal choices? What about in politics?

- Who are the key people you admire who engage politically? Why do you admire them?

- What books, essays, documentaries, or other media inform how you engage or disengage from political discussion about [insert your topic here]?

- What do you want to know concerning people who disagree with you about [insert your topic here]?

- What do you want people who might disagree with your perspectives on political topics to know about you?

LIE 6

THE AMERICAN DREAM IS ALIVE AND WELL

THE AMERICAN DREAM IS POPULARLY DEFINED as the "ideal that every US citizen should have an equal opportunity to achieve success and prosperity through hard work, determination, and initiative." At least that's what came up when I put it into Google. I absorbed this idea at an early age. I realized that if I worked hard, I would be praised, accepted and even coveted as a partner, friend, and mate. Conversely, if I was lazy, I would be criticized, ridiculed, and abandoned. Thus, I avoided being perceived as lazy, lacking initiative, or not striving to fulfill my potential because of the fear of being cast away. This is not just a personal fear of mine; it was reinforced in my family and environment. Being successful and prosperous was how I earned a place to belong. They were not just ideals to strive for but a sort of initiation rite into the club of productive members of society.

I didn't learn this just from *It's a Wonderful Life*, *The Brady Bunch*, or even watching *Family Matters* Friday nights on ABC. I learned it from my family through passing comments, disapproving glances, and arguments I overheard when I wasn't supposed to be listening. Home planted the seeds, and society made sure they grew through my fear of being seen as lazy and unproductive, a stereotype rooted in the African American experience. It is a terrible sin in white American folk religion for any ethnic group to be lazy, but it is unforgivable to be a "lazy black man" in the United States. After being called a n—— and prejudged as angry and dangerous, the assumption that I am lazy, unwilling, or unable to work is the next most crippling label for men who look like me. I doubt there is any message so ingrained in my mind than to "work hard." No doubt, every American ethnic group has faced the command to work and contribute in order to earn their place, but it is different for the descendants of slaves, whose very worth was based on their usefulness to a slave master, quantified in terms of dollars and cents.

Still, the American dream can feel slippery and hard to define. To capture its ethos is like trying to quantify the impact and importance of the air Americans breathe. There are several gases in the air, but there is one chief element and result. The element is oxygen and the result is life itself. The air in most of the United States is 78 percent nitrogen and 20 percent oxygen. Hard work is the oxygen and sustaining force behind the American dream, yet when we actually examine the lives of those who are "successful," the majority of their experiences and triumphs have little to do with their hard work. Other elements are in the air.

In the early days of the United States, these other elements explicitly dominated the environment. WAFR was and still is the nitrogen. Bias, whether unconscious or not, looms much larger than one's own efforts, but in the narrative of the American dream, hard work, like oxygen, is the focus and deemed the most important and beneficial element of success.

We see this in oft-repeated phrases like "He is a self-made man" and "She pulled herself up by her own bootstraps." Those who "make it" are celebrated, praised, and affirmed for their individual efforts. In the context of America's history of genocide, enslavement, and entrenched racial and gender bias, both of these statements are absurd. But they are attractive and enticing. Job, pay, and loan discrimination, along with barriers to education and access to housing, made it nearly impossible for the protected to fail and those in the margins to succeed. Therefore, the American dream, a logical outworking of WAFR, is the widest and most deeply held belief by those who live out of this un-Christian faith.

A DREAM BUILT ON PRIDE AND IDOLATRY

The American dream is troublesome for the previously mentioned reasons and, most importantly, because it points to the cardinal sins of pride and idolatry. The doctrine of America calls for the self to be exalted and one's name to be made famous. Additionally, we should be made in the likenesses of WAFR's most successful people. This collection of individuals is nothing more than an updated version of Babel. At the ancient city of Babel, they said, "Come, let us build for ourselves a city, and a tower whose top *will reach* into heaven, and let us make for ourselves a name" (Genesis 11:4).

Followers of WAFR, like those who had Babel built for them, are not interested in worshiping Yahweh but instead themselves. To maintain dominance, WAFR has co-opted genuine Christianity. It relies on holding grace through Christ in one hand and working for one's identity and prosperity as truth in the other. This twisted hypocrisy is ultimately destructive.

Jesus said, "You cannot serve God and wealth" (Matthew 6:24). Yet in America, god *is* money, so there seems to be no problem with acquiring it. WAFR has no issue with walking in hypocrisy. In short, WAFR calls this wholehearted dedication to personal pleasure and comfort at all costs "following Jesus," because all we have to do is thank him when we get the Grammy, MVP award, or bonus check—and we are *good*. Just give 10 percent to the church and show up on time to Sunday gatherings twice a month. These supposed overtures to god are not what Christ requires but are certainly necessary for the façade of WAFR and the veneer of this "Christian" nation.

This is not just the story of America; it stretches around the world. WAFR is embedded in the American psyche and exported to every corner of the planet through media, merchandise, and the military. The message heard around the world, and the ideal goal of many countries, is to be a place where it's true that *no matter where you come from, with hard work anyone can improve their life. All you need is a chance to try*. And America provides the most equal footing and the most opportunities to strive for all the pleasure and possessions our efforts can afford.

It is these well-exported ideas that drove my good friend Shandra to trust a human trafficker in her home country of Indonesia posing as a recruiter for US hotels. Shandra was educated, intelligent, and longed for more opportunity. Her family was not poor, but seeing her limited opportunities, she gave money to this agent of exploitation for a ticket to America.

In her own words, she wanted McDonald's, Pizza Hut, and the life she saw in the movies. That's what was sold to her, and she bought it.

Upon arrival in the United States, she was supposed to change flights and head to Chicago. But instead Shandra was told there was a misunderstanding and she would need to spend a night at the Sheraton Hotel in Flushing, Queens. Once there, she was transferred at gunpoint and threats of violence from one man to another and then sold for sex in casinos, hotels, and brothels fronting as massage parlors in Connecticut, the five NYC boroughs, and New Jersey. The American dream quickly became a nightmare that only Christ and community could free her from. She learned that the American dream isn't just false, but its promises are never fulfilled. It is most often in dire circumstances that we see the true hand of exploitative capitalism and spiritual poverty at work. The original sins of this nation still occur but are hidden so that America won't be blamed, shamed, or held responsible.

It is difficult to detect the impact of these twisted values in our everyday lives. Just as high levels of carbon dioxide will be found if we have the right equipment when we look up from our toil, we see the tragic effect of a nation pursuing gain at any cost.

A DREAM BUILT ON LABOR AND SEXUAL EXPLOITATION

Human traffickers are much like the slave traders, colonists, and explorers who long ago landed on the shores of what we now call Africa, the Americas, Asia, and the Caribbean. These men and women were not there to give life, dignity, and respect to those they encountered. Their sole purpose was to make money and acquire as much wealth and comfort for themselves as possible. It is painfully false to think that the British, French, and other colonizing nations sent their ships for anything other than the expansion of their own wealth, influence, and security.

It is even more offensive to the oppressed and marginalized to rebrand their abuse, exploitation, and violence as heroic and inspiring. This happened when Christopher Columbus became a hero. A US national holiday honors his supposed bravery while dismissing the atrocities he committed in the name of money and power. This also happens when certain Christians dismiss Jonathan Edwards's support of slavery or harsh racism of the Puritans. And this happens most subtly every day when we celebrate CEOs and business owners who knowingly exploit those in their supply chains in every corner of the world. Yet their faces appear on magazine covers, their voices are heard on podcasts, and their names are honored by business schools.

Two of the most powerful companies in the United States today are Walmart and Apple. Both of their founders, Sam Walton and Steve Jobs respectively, are touted as emblematic of the American dream. Walton created the largest retail store in the world, starting in the small town of Bentonville, Arkansas; Jobs, adopted as an infant child of Syrian lineage, founded the most valuable company in American history (by worldly standards).[1]

What these men did for us is deemed most valuable. And we need to know how they did it so we can do it too. WAFR and those under its influence dehumanize human beings and reduce people made in the image of God to their individual efforts and usefulness. This is why, when a TV host like Bill O'Reilly, an entertainer like Bill Cosby, or a coach like Joe Paterno participates in or covers up sexual violence, our first inclination is to protect them and their institutions—not those they have violated. These men actually *become* their work, their efforts and their contributions to society. They model the success on the surface that epitomizes the pursuit of life, liberty, and happiness at all costs. As Donald Trump put it so clearly about his inability to resist sexually harassing women: "You know I'm automatically attracted to beautiful—I just start kissing them. It's like a magnet. Just kiss. I don't even wait. . . . And when you're a star they let you do it. You can do anything . . . grab them by the p—. You can do anything."[2]

And then Americans elected him president.

WAFR is not concerned with personal and social integrity but is fundamentally protective of its institutions. Therefore, when a trespass is discovered, only those arguments and narratives that protect the status quo will rise to the surface. Calls for change are pushed to the edges and drowned out by those in power. Or, in the case of Harvey Weinstein at Miramax and Roger Ailes at Fox News, they are pushed out to protect the institution and those who benefit from it.[3]

Similarly, to the vast majority of the world, Jobs and Walton are not individuals made in God's image. They are solely identified by their work. Sam Walton is Walmart and Steve Jobs is Apple. Our identities become our greatest accomplishments, and conversely our mistakes become our greatest liabilities. Fortunately, there are glaring differences between this way of life and the kingdom of the risen Jesus. Peter's encounters with Jesus show that the money we make, the occupations we hold, and the social status those things provide do not determine our identity, worth, and value.

LEAVE THE DREAM BEHIND

In Luke 5:1-11, we see Peter's encounter with Jesus. This is Peter's moment of profound obedience, courage, and faith. First, in response to Jesus' entering his fishing boat, Peter pushes out from shore and allows Jesus to teach the crowd. Second, Peter is willing to push farther from shore even after he had fished all night with no success. Peter was likely exhausted and discouraged. If there were no fish, he would have no food and no income. And now here was Jesus, a carpenter's son, telling Peter, a fisherman who knows his trade, to go into deeper water and drop his now clean nets in the middle of the day where no fish would be anyway. Peter knows this isn't the best time or place to fish, but he obeys.

And because of his obedience, Peter witnesses a miracle. At a time and in a place where it made no human sense for him to catch fish, there are more fish than he can carry to shore, and he has to ask for help.

In WAFR under the banner of the American dream, Peter would try to hire Jesus and compliment him on his natural talents and abilities for catching fish. Or perhaps he would interview Jesus or try to get his three-step process for what to do when he can't catch fish. At a minimum, in the American dream, Peter would have taken the fish to market and cashed in on this great catch. But instead Peter takes a step of courage. He leaves his business, training, income, and all that comes with that to be with and learn the ways of God from Jesus. By faith, he puts down his nets and accepts the invitation to become a fisher of humans and one of Jesus' disciples.

Steps like this profoundly confuse those fully invested in the American dream. Upon graduating from Columbia, I told billionaire entrepreneur John Kluge that I would be coming on staff with Inter-Varsity Christian Fellowship to direct the New York City Urban Project. Bear in mind that between 2006 and 2008, John had purchased more than six hundred copies of my books of poetry to share with his family, friends, and colleagues. He and his wife had sponsored spoken-word workshops and performances with schools, prisons, and churches. He shared honestly that he thought this job wasn't a good idea and offered to connect me with publishers to continue to grow my career and platform in writing.

I considered his advice and wrestled with what it would mean to raise financial support and live dependent on God and other people for my provision. I struggled with saying no to becoming famous and the idea of exchanging performing in front of fans with sitting in front of fidgety college students. Ultimately though, no matter how I sloshed it around in my brain, the choice was between doing what I was good at and utilizing my gifts for my own comfort and benefit, or being who God called me to be and walking in obedience to Christ. I believe this invitation from God in 2008 set the stage for him to speak clearly to me in 2011 to commit twenty years to his work through me in InterVarsity. I said yes, but not because I believed it was the best idea and would maximize my personal growth and impact. I responded like Peter in Luke 5:5, "I will do as You say."

Now, if this was the American dream at work, I would give three action steps to be faithful, obedient, and courageous in your own life. But the beginning, middle, and end of this story are about Jesus and what he is doing in the world. The gospel of Jesus Christ is not a road map to "my best life now." It is Christ crucified, buried, and raised from the dead that we might have an eternal place in an eternal family.

Peter's story continues with not only faithfulness and courage, but also disobedience to and rejection of Jesus. We see these difficult moments in Luke 22:54-62. Here the Gospel writer recounts Peter's denials of his relationship with, allegiance to, and knowledge of Christ.

Earlier in Luke 22, Jesus said he prayed that Peter's faith would be strengthened to withstand Satan's challenges. Peter asserted that he would follow Jesus to prison and even death. Peter's assertion is met with a predictive rebuke, "I say to you, Peter, the rooster will not crow today until you have denied three times that you know Me" (Luke 22:34).

The next day Jesus was in a vulnerable position, surrounded by enemies, betrayed by a friend, and certainly about to be put to death. And Peter, the rock on which the church is to be built, denies its Cornerstone, Jesus Christ himself—not just once but three times, just as Jesus had said he would.

Similarly, after I received the invitation from Jesus to join Inter-Varsity and commit to twenty years of service, I regularly succumbed to fear and addiction. For years my stress was managed not by prayer but by pornography. If I felt disappointed, lonely, and out of control, I went to PornTube, not Bible Gateway. After pornography, my next vice was food. When I couldn't solve problems or figure out conflict, late-night meals were my escape. But because of my body-image issues, the guilt about stress eating often led to diets that I called "fasts" along with lofty workout goals such as 5Ks and marathons, which left my feet and ankles injured and in need of surgery. I was gifted and broken, talented and tainted, following a perfect Jesus so imperfectly but striving nonetheless.

If Peter were in America and WAFR was in control, this would have been the end of his career (and mine as well). We would no doubt be let go and likely have never been hired if our trespasses were somehow known beforehand. This type of brand damage would not be written about and sent to every member of our churches or the shareholders of our companies. The scandal would be hidden, and an email or press release would be sent about the pending "transition" that was effective immediately. But because the kingdom of God comes close to us in the person of Jesus, Christ exercises the power that he has to confer an identity on us that is rooted in a place that is unshakeable. Our actions don't determine our place at his table; his act of sacrificing himself confirms our seat.

THE LIFE YOU GAIN

Timothy and Sarah Buxton laid down their nets as well. Priscilla and I went to a sale at their Washington Heights apartment and bought Corningware, a globe, and a mirror that hangs in our dining room. The small amount of funds from that sale helped send their family to Iraq. In the years to come, they would raise their three children in the shadow of ISIS and create refuge for thousands of people fleeing war and violence—all because they said yes to Jesus.

Maria and Sean Blackburn put down their nets too. They left Long Island to work with Nomi Network in Phnom Penh, taking the work they had done to serve youth on this side of the world to the other so that the scourge of sex-trafficking and labor slavery doesn't have the last say in the lives of a growing number of young women and men in Cambodia. Ricky and Courtney Bolander left their jobs in New York City and followed Jesus to Romania to love and support vulnerable girls in the orphanages and impoverished communities through their NGO, Radiant Hope. Jimmy Lee left the world of finance so he could lead Restore NYC in order to more deeply love neighbors who were vulnerable to exploitation; and Ben and Heather remain in finance, leveraging their resources to reflect the kingdom of God in boardrooms and business meetings throughout the world.

Leaving your nets might look like changing your career or moving around the corner or around the world. It might look like staying exactly where you are, but it requires reorienting your heart and wrapping your life around the will of God because of his love and by his grace.

Jesus invited his disciples into a totally different value system, and that invitation is extended to us today. As long as we worship productivity, live out of the fear of disappointing others, and pursue personal glory and gain, we cannot seek his kingdom first. Jesus said, "whoever loses their life will preserve it" (Luke 17:33 NIV); that is not the message we are told in the United States. The lie that we are our work is powerfully attractive and profoundly untrue. We must put down our nets and follow Jesus the way Peter did in order to become his children and truly live.

QUESTIONS FOR INDIVIDUAL REFLECTION AND SMALL GROUP DISCUSSION

- What were your dominant feelings as you read this chapter: curiosity, hope, surprise, confusion, numbness, familiarity, distance, or something else?

- When were those feelings most present?

- What phrases, stories, or historical events resonated with you?

- What events or narratives were you unaware of? What did you learn?

- Where do you disagree or have concerns?

- What questions are you carrying?

WHAT IS YOUR NET AND WHAT IS JESUS ASKING YOU TO DO?

- Is there a person, group of people, or plan that is more important to you than following Jesus?

- What are you afraid of losing or fear would happen if you were to change your profession/career, not get married, not have children, or do the opposite?

- What things might be said about you by your family, friends, or culture if you changed jobs, moved away, didn't get married, married "her," went to "that" church, or gave away that much money?

- If you were not afraid and had all of the resources in the world at your disposal, a clear word from Jesus, and the support of your community—what would you do to bear witness to the glory of God?

LIE 7

WE ARE THE MOST PROSPEROUS NATION IN THE WORLD

HER GRAVESTONE SAID, "August 24, 1952–September 13, 2015."
Seeing the date written out like that made it so final. Ma was gone. I
realize now that I judged her and her choices. I said in front of crowds
and in private conversations that the life she provided for us was "poor,"
and I subconsciously hoped that she would come to see the city and the
university she sent me to as more valuable than the place she sent me
from. I did not know that was going to be one of the outcomes of my
education, and I am disappointed that I could draw such a conclusion
about the woman who raised me and the place she reared me in.

I wanted Ma to see jazz and ballet at Lincoln Center, hear poetry at
the Nuyorican cafe, and smell the autumn air in a stroll down the
Museum Mile to the Met while tasting different flavors of gelato. I
wanted her to experience what is supposed to be the richest congres-
sional district in the country, taking a break from one of the poorest
places in America. She responded that she liked her simple life.

As I sat in Grand Central Station writing these words on my laptop,
I thought about how Ma knew something about being rich that econ-
omists and my humanities professors missed. I remembered the
words that echoed in my mind as she slipped from life to death and
life again with God: "What will it profit a man if he gains the whole
world, and loses his own soul?" (Mark 8:36 NKJV).

PROFIT AND PROSPERITY

Profit, gain, prosperity: all synonyms for what historians say America has amassed more of than any country in human history. Yet this again is a claim rooted in the sands of white American folk religion, not the rock of the kingdom of God. It is a lie that the attainment of the American dream makes us truly wealthy.

After Jesus said that he must be crucified, Peter attempted to get Jesus to change his mind. Later, though, Peter confessed that Jesus truly is the Christ. Jesus then says,

> What good is it for someone to gain the whole world, yet forfeit their soul? Or what can anyone give in exchange for their soul? If anyone is ashamed of me and my words in this adulterous and sinful generation, the Son of Man will be ashamed of them when he comes in his Father's glory with the holy angels. (Mark 8:36-38 NIV)

What does it profit me to gain access to wealth, fame, status, elite education, and higher rungs on social and economic ladders at the expense of my own health and well-being and of those around me? What do I truly acquire from this world when its offer is ultimately meaningless and separates me from those I love on this side of eternity and Jesus on the other? The cost to follow Jesus is high, yet the reward is infinitely greater. The cost of worshiping money and pursuing pleasure is also high, yet the reward is fleeting, finite, and temporary.

As I looked at Ma's gravestone and considered my family members that I was parted from while I was working for better economic and educational opportunities, I asked myself, *What did I leave this place for?*

The answer was clearer than ever: WAFR; specifically, the American dream and the prosperity it promised. I left to pursue a false prosperity that centered on my own wants and needs, not on Christ's kingdom and his righteousness.

Looking back, I also can see that I left because every person I met told me that I had to. My leaving was not just some personal project but an intricate part of the social fabric that I come from. African Americans have long fought for access to the wealth and prosperity of America. So, it's no mystery that the migration for opportunity and resources existed when I was in high school and persists strongly to this day.

Though most people I knew had not been where I was going, they told me I had to get out. It was as though my talents with words and sports qualified me for release from the prison of Brodnax, Mecklenburg County, southern Virginia—and from the South altogether. I didn't question it when I opened the letter with confetti inside and then bought my train ticket on credit to visit Columbia University. I didn't question it because I was told that I would adjust. I was shocked when I arrived in August 2004. I could not fathom how people lived the way they do in a big city—millions packed into tiny spaces where rich and poor strive to make a life out of giving up as little time and money as possible to gain as much time and money as they can. This was the rat race, and now it was my turn and my privilege to run. This race was a good thing, I was told by family, friends, admissions officers, and "good Christians." So, I ran and didn't ask many questions. I am still running today because I am unsure of how to stop.

CHOOSING BETWEEN JESUS AND SOMETHING ELSE

We who ascribe consciously or unconsciously to WAFR's tenets have moments of striking clarity when the ramifications of our beliefs rise to the surface and must be faced. Mine come every moment I reflect on my momma's life and death. The inconsistency in what I say and what I value brings tears to my eyes. How could I do that to her? And not just to my momma but to my aunts and uncles, and my church family that loved me as best they could with unwavering support.

I will never forget the kindness of Ms. Thomason. I had put together a puzzle for my momma of the Manhattan skyline and wanted to frame it to go in her living room in Brodnax. So I went to Thomason's frameshop, but when I got out of the car, the wind caught the edge of the cardboard I had mounted it on and 20 percent of Manhattan blew onto the ground. Thomason and I sat at her counter for an hour talking and putting the puzzle back together. She had time for that, and she had time for me. She also took the only $20 bill from her register and gave it to me to support my work with InterVarsity in New York City. The same would be true of Uncle Marvin, Robin, and Glenn at Dogwood Graphics and Louis Blackwell at Meherrin Baptist Church and the hours' worth of conversations they had with me. These people lead rich, deep lives, and my leaving to get the "best" was not supposed to mean that I saw their wealth and depth as deficient and impoverished because it was different from what I was now taught to value. I was not supposed to become educated so that I could say others were ignorant, backward, or stupid. I was not supposed to succeed in a city so that I could insult folks who lived in small towns and suburbs.

It is possible to live a meaningful life in loving service to God and other people in Brodnax, Virginia. Simultaneously, it is also possible to live in New York City and live a life of purpose and beauty.

But this is not what the lie of American prosperity and its interconnected myth about the American dream would have me or any other person on this planet believe. The idol never outs itself. Because if we stop to question the race to acquire material wealth, then the house of cards falls apart.

One name for this house of cards is GDP (Gross Domestic Product). The United States makes a convincing and attractive case based on the sheer financial holdings of its citizen worshipers of WAFR. It makes the proclamation that this type of life is good for all people. At the turn of World War II, with much of the world in disarray, the United States accounted for 50 percent of the world economic output, cementing its monetary dominance.[1] Decades later, the United States still holds 25 percent of global output and the largest economy. Closer to home, the US median household income per year is about $60,000, while it's $27,000 in the United Kingdom, and $8,000 in Brazil. *Scientific American* puts it most clearly:

> With less than 5 percent of world population, the U.S. uses one-third of the world's paper, a quarter of the world's oil, 23 percent of the coal, 27 percent of the aluminum, and 19 percent of the copper. . . . Our per capita use of energy, metals, minerals, forest products, fish, grains, meat, and even fresh water dwarfs that of people living in the developing world.[2]

These numbers are striking because if life, liberty, and comfort are America's goals, then we have little competition. If prosperity is our ability to buy and dispose of 140 million cell phones and 300 million pairs of shoes annually, and eat $14.3 billion dollars' worth of chocolate per year, then we are winning the race.[3] From the perspective of WAFR, it makes no sense that Peter would leave his fishing business to follow Jesus or for Matthew to stop collecting taxes and give away four times what he had taken. For these two men, following Jesus was an explicit invitation to stop following the evil influence of material wealth. Here is where the sin of greediness rises to the surface of WAFR.

THE ILLUSION OF "MAKING IT" IN AMERICA

Greed is not exclusive to America, but the cultural adoption, social validation, and societal prodding for more in the United States is unprecedented. Not only is selfish ambition promoted, it is unapologetically projected onto every successive generation with more force. Tim Keller, founding pastor of Redeemer Presbyterian Church in New York City, says,

> As a pastor, I've had people come to me and confess that they struggle with almost every kind of sin. Almost. I cannot recall anyone ever coming to me and saying, "I spend too much money on myself. I think my greedy lust for money is harming my family, my soul, and people around me."[4]

WAFR invites us to wealth and status measurable in dollars and cents, and a personal paradise defined exclusively by our own efforts plus talents and chance. The invitation is to practice the same sin that put African slaves on ships and drove Native Americans to reservations. Jesus calls us to forsake the comforts of this world and live in the kingdom of heaven where we lack nothing because we have the Son of God. This is true riches according to the Holy Scriptures, yet to have only Christ is poverty according to the framers of the US Constitution.

As followers of Jesus experience true prosperity on this side of heaven as a result of not bowing to the idol of wealth, those who fall outside of the pursuit of comfort by choice, failure, or force are pressed to the edges of our culture and consciousness so as not to interrupt production in the American marketplace.

There is the illusion that "we all have it made in America" and "we all have a shot to make it in America." This appears to be true because our country hides those who haven't "made it" (or refuse to try) from those who have and are presently running the race. Many Native Americans live in exclusion on reservations, in sparsely populated areas, or were forced to assimilate, leaving their culture behind. Jim Crow laws along with loan, mortgage, and insurance discrimination based on race are slowly scrubbed from public education materials, and any media highlighting present-day racism are dismissed as isolated incidents. Mass incarceration, unjust education policies, and other tools for segregation and subjugation are dismissed as mere theories because "look at the success of Oprah and Obama." Immigrants are criminalized, forced to assimilate and exchange their ethnic identity for whiteness, or remain on the outside subject to ridicule, prejudice, physical violence, or abuse of power.

Moreover, Americans of European descent who lack higher education and financial resources too often live in neglected suburbs, public housing, or rural communities increasingly fraught with suicide, addiction, high incarceration rates, and vulnerability to corporate exploitation via low-wage jobs. Even the wealthy hide debt and maintain lifestyles they can't afford by using credit to keep up appearances.

Under WAFR, wealth and work communicate the value of a person, and the faithfulness of a person is measured by their contribution to the economy. Wealth is blessed and work is worshiped. If I am not perceived to be bringing my offering, then I am a "taker," a "welfare queen/king," that is lazy and entitled. If I accumulate or inherit wealth and power, then I am a "maker," a "job creator," and someone to be celebrated, revered, and protected. Without reflection, this is an enticing idea for those without means. No wonder those around me at Park View High School told me to go as far and as fast as I could. It was sobering for me to believe the lie that we are all created equal and then realize that I had been placed in an arena to jockey for social position while suffering under a centuries-long system of intentional handicap.

TRUE WEALTH

It is true that the United States has accumulated more financial resources than any nation in history. It is also true that it is spiritually bankrupt and devoid of purpose and vision outside the pursuit of more security, stability, and material wealth. WAFR leaves all parties wanting. But the people of God lack nothing (Psalm 23). Followers of WAFR—pursuing the American dream—are not truly prosperous because their souls are owned by an idol made with human hands off the backs of other humans. This pursuit will never satisfy their deepest needs. Jesus comes into this reality and offers freedom and an abundant life with him.

As my mother lay dying, I did not quote Plato's *Republic* or pontificate on Emerson's existentialist musings. I did not try to leverage my connections to get better treatment, or charm the doctors and nurses for extra care. Instead, my family and I sang the songs of slaves who knew what true freedom was and served the Master of the universe rather than the master with the whip. Jesus said,

> Do not store up for yourselves [material] treasures on earth, where moths and vermin destroy, and where thieves break in

and steal. But store up for yourselves treasures in heaven, where moths and vermin do not destroy, and where thieves do not break in and steal. For where your treasure is, there your heart [your wishes, your desires; what your life is centered on] will be also. (Matthew 6:19-21 NIV, with my additions)

There was no question where my momma's riches were invested. Because she died in Christ, she will share in his resurrection. This indescribable wealth is the desire and inheritance of the Christian, and it shines in beautiful, victorious opposition to the bent knees of WAFR.

QUESTIONS FOR INDIVIDUAL REFLECTION AND SMALL GROUP DISCUSSION

- What were your dominant feelings as you read this chapter: curiosity, hope, surprise, confusion, numbness, familiarity, distance, or something else?
- When were those feelings most present?
- What phrases, stories, or historical events resonated with you?
- What events or narratives were you unaware of? What did you learn?
- Where do you disagree or have concerns?
- What questions are you carrying?

WHAT ARE YOUR CORE BELIEFS ABOUT FINANCIAL WEALTH AND MATERIAL POVERTY?

- What do your parents and grandparents believe about people who have little savings or financial wealth?
- Conversely, what do they believe about people who do have material wealth and resources?
- What do your closest friends believe about those who own homes or rent in "better" neighborhoods?

- What do your family and closest friends believe about people with large debts, or who receive welfare, or live on social security?

- How do you see individuals and families who suffer from material poverty, or live in impoverished areas, or live in "developing" nations?

- How would your self-esteem and the way you see yourself change if you lost your job and savings, and had no way of making an income?

- How would you change your life to become rich in the things of God and not the things of this world?

RESPONSE

Sin is personal, relational, and systemic. Something might not be our fault but it is our responsibility.

If you, your family, or people group consistently judge those you perceive to have less and you think about or treat them differently, you have not honored the image of God in them and need to lament, confess, repent, and seek reconciliation.

If you, your family, or people group have consistently built your identity around financial wealth and material possessions, you are bowing to idols and need to confess, repent, and seek reconciliation.

Take a moment to write your own prayers of confession. If you need help, here is an example.

Gracious God, in Christ Jesus, you teach us to love our neighbors but instead we build dividing walls of hostility. You show us how to love one another as sisters and brothers but instead we hide from our own human family. You ask us to seek out the stranger and welcome the guest. You want us to share your abundant gifts with the poor but instead we cling tightly to our possessions and our privilege. You call us to proclaim good news to all people but instead we waste our words and hide our light. Lord, our loving God, have mercy on us. Forgive our sin, open our hearts, and change our lives. Fill us with the Holy Spirit. Make us holy and whole—one people, united in faith, hope, and love through Jesus Christ, Our reconciler and redeemer.[5]

After you have prayed this prayer of confession, ask someone to pray this prayer of blessing over you, because after confession there is always blessing. Jesus doesn't send us away but instead sends us out to bear witness to and for him!

In the name of the Father, the Son, and the Holy Spirit, you, brother or sister, are blessed and sent as a seeker of shalom and justice for the powerful and the powerless, the oppressed and the oppressors, the privileged and the marginalized, and all people made in the image of God. You have been reconciled to God by the blood of Christ Jesus and filled with Holy Spirit. You are therefore Christ's ambassador, called to call all to be reconciled to him and one another by the name of the risen Lamb that reconciled you. Be blessed between the now and the not yet to preach and practice the ways of Jesus, making sacred space for those in your care to be loved through sacred listening and Christ-centered spirit-led activism. Like Moses, you have been sent to Pharaoh to make Yahweh known so that Egyptians and Israelites may worship in spirit and in truth, now and for always. By his grace, through the gift of faith and for his glory. Amen!

LIE 8

WE ARE THE MOST GENEROUS PEOPLE IN THE WORLD

In 2003, I put on a suit, got in my truck, and went to Peebles Corporation. I wanted to ask for money to help publish my first book. I was sixteen, had written a book of poems, and wanted to print it. So my mom and I, along with a mentor named Marcy McDonald, made phone calls, got on the internet, and tried to find out how much it would cost to design and print. After lots of conversations, Brunswick Publishing told us it would cost around $15,000 to print twelve hundred copies. That was a lot of money. It was more than my family made in a year.

To put this in a financial context, I worked for little more than $5.15 per hour that year while in high school. Those around me made similar wages, meaning that a full-time job would give a person around $10,000 a year before taxes—if the job lasted the entire year. My mom worked three jobs and made little more than $20,000 a year, and that was true of nearly every person I knew. This is not the best context for art and poetry to have the space to grow and thrive. This is the place where dreams of creativity can die beneath the need to eat, pay for electricity, and care for children, the sick, and the aged. There is little margin here, and bankruptcy, payday loans, and buying gas by the gallon is normal. I admit that I now understand this in hindsight because my teenage mind was unaware of the true state of things around me.

I approached many local businesses, asking for help. I sat down in front of Carolyn Blackwell at Peebles Corporation and told her what I was trying to do. Peebles was one of the largest employers in town and our only true department store with a local distribution center. They wrote a check that paid for the book to be set for the printer. Looking back, going to all of these businesses and asking them to give money to publish a book of poems made very little sense, but in Mecklenburg County, with a backdrop of cyclical poverty and a significant opportunity gap, efforts like mine take investment from the entire community. Material poverty necessitated regular dependence on a larger community for daily survival. Interdependence was not a concept but a lived reality.

Gloria Taylor, branch director of the local library, donated her time to paint an original cover for the book. And Dogwood Graphics gave me a discount to set the book for printing. My mom refinanced the land we lived on and came up with the remainder of the funds to take *My Release* from a stack of papers to a hardback book.

In spite of all of those efforts, to ask those around us who couldn't afford much to buy a book for fifteen dollars made very little financial sense. Yet we sold all those books before I left for Columbia in the fall of 2004, and we printed another thousand paperback copies that sold out as well. It bears repeating that the people of my area were financially limited, and much of my personal success is the result of my mother's sacrifice and the financial investment of black and white materially poor Americans. This was my lens for generosity—relational and sacrificial. These people were most often not able to give, but they did anyway. Little did I know, I would meet people not two years later who made in a day what my family did in a year.

My junior year in college I went to Weehawken, New Jersey. I was going to visit my friend's father, who worked at the United Bank of Switzerland (UBS). I knew nothing about UBS before I visited. The financial services industry, especially in New York City, was a complete and utter mystery to me. His office was massive, and at the time I didn't know what an office on such a high floor meant. I was distinctly out of my element but was in that room because of my passion for ending human trafficking and sexual exploitation of children in northern Uganda. I don't remember all that was said, but I left that meeting with a check to support the ministry.

The following week I got on a plane for the first time in my life and headed to Palm Beach, Florida, with other students to meet John Kluge. I did not know my meeting him was part of Columbia University's effort to secure the largest gift in the history of the institution and the largest gift ever for students from backgrounds like mine to have access to elite education. His pledge would be $400 million.[1] Over lunch on the second day of our trip, he asked each student to share their passions. I shared about my advocacy against human trafficking in Uganda and my desire to see an end to the use of children as soldiers and sex slaves, using my poem about Jacob and victims of exploitation and violence in northern Uganda:

> I'm breathing in the last breathes of the Acholi
> running with Jacob as he flees Joseph Coney
> bleeding, wheezing, maimed, and beaten
> wheezing I'm bleeding, blameless but beaten
> beaten and bleeding, coughing and wheezing
> breathing in the last of the Acholi
> See Jacob—he is part of the Acholi Tribe
> and he is just one invisible child
> a faceless name with forty thousand others just like him
> a nameless face as you see him on advertisements . . . See Jacob
> He walks eight miles looking back all the while
> because another child soldier could attack and kidnap
> and he will be forced to trade his backpack
> for an AK-47 and an army knapsack
> Fear is the rebels' main weapon
> and they spread death like an infection
> so children are paralyzed, no threat of an insurrection
> Ages 8-14, boys are given guns
> and girls are simply given to someone
> I close my eyes and in the streets I am sleeping

trying to wake up from this dream
I can't believe this is happening to me . . .
I wake up
but Jacob never does
because this nightmare is his lifemare
that I can't dream through, that I can't sleep through
but he walks through, talks through,
and praises God all through
I am looking at a blank page
trying to paint the faces of invisible individuals
with my words
Trying to capture a reality
that my mind can't grasp with a pen and a pad
I'm trying to be that poet that writes that poem
that actually does this story justice
But I've seen that documentary
not once, not twice, but nine times three
and it's on permanent repeat in my mind's TV
I hear Jacob saying I would rather be dead
see a crying priest draw a cross from his heart to his head
see an entire country drowning in bloodshed
I don't want to see another Hotel Rwanda
I don't want to see another swollen belly from Somalia
I don't want to see another photo from the Congo
I don't want to see these invisible children so I don't.
They are invisible to me, invisible to us
invisible to everyone because we've intentionally chosen
not to acknowledge their humanity
Tony said "Don't forget about me,
don't forget about me."
Lock me in the vaults of your memory
replay my face every day and remember me
remember me

I am looking at a blank page filled with words
unworthy to tell Jacob's story
but I kept my promise that I took
when I walked with him when I talked with him
"Don't forget me," Tony said—and I can't
because they are the only things that I remember[2]

Looking back, I don't think that's what they were expecting. Shortly after I shared this piece, Kluge's wife pulled me to the side and decided to donate her Christmas gift to the work that I was doing. She handed me a check. I was dumbfounded and a few minutes later I asked if she was sure, because the amount matched the one I had received the week before. She laughed and said, "Of course." I was unaware that I was standing on an estate twice the size of the Mar-a-Lago estate next to it.

Now with more money in my bank account than I had ever seen, and with the sole purpose of giving it away as effectively as I could, I was ushered into the world of philanthropy. In this space of excess, expensive auctions are held with well-dressed men and women sipping cocktails around dinner tables while a master of ceremony asks for $25,000 via the wave of a paddle, and volunteers rush over with iPads to turn pledges into real money. This was a different world for me, one that I lost in translation. At one point I found myself—in sweatpants, an undershirt, and a backpack—at the World Vision office at 29th and 7th in Manhattan being given two large checks. From the outset when I stepped off the elevator, I was not quite sure what George Ross, Kirsten Stearns, Rahsaan Graham, Sweena Varghese, Patricia Holmes, or Sharon Park thought of me, but I later spent long hours hanging out in their offices. I was never an intern, not quite an employee, sometimes an independent contractor, and most often an artist associate—but more important than my position was that I was always welcome. And it was that type of Allen Road community (my home community) that I recognized and relished. In that season of generosity, I gained so much more than I gave. I am a witness that Acts 20:35 is true: "It is more blessed to give than to receive."

I say this with conviction because two years later, in May 2008, I sat with my mom around the same boardroom table at the World Vision offices with the same friends she prayed I would meet. I remember my mom and aunt sleeping in the master bedroom of the Jackson family home during my graduation weekend, and sipping tea at the dinner table across from John Kluge that summer. My mom embodied the sacrificial generosity of an entire community that blessed and sent me to NYC with faith in God and my poems, and the staff at World Vision, along with the Jacksons and Kluges, embodied some of the best efforts to steward wealth to love our neighbors with much less, including me.

These two groups of people—the materially wealthy and well-connected, and the materially poor and geographically isolated—taught me what generosity looks like and helped me unlearn my assumptions about socioeconomic classes in America. I am blessed to know people who prove there are radical exceptions to the rules of the poverty, greed, and the hoarding (or lack of) resources and opportunity that is the hallmark of WAFR and its reign in this country.

I am deeply grateful to God for the sacrifices my mom made for me to leave Brodnax. At the same time I know that our predicament is downstream of slavery, Jim Crow laws, and racial and gender discrimination. If justice had rolled down like a mighty stream in America, our story would be very different. Nevertheless, I am enormously appreciative of the compassion and generosity of the Kluges and the Jacksons. But I hold in tension that the advantages these families enjoy are in part because of the laws, policies, and social norms of the United States. Their generosity went against the accepted tide of socially acceptable giving; it did not flow with it. Thanks be to God.

Both groups—one side in Brodnax, Virginia, and the other in Palm Beach and Manhattan, are compassionate compared to their cultural counterparts. But their compassion is no match for the generosity of our Father, Christ, and Holy Spirit. Thus my mom's sacrifice and the compassion of the Jacksons and Kluges do not reflect a world where things are working rightly. They are reminders and testimonies that things are not working as God intended. They are a rebuke of the American narrative of personal pleasure and comfort at the expense of others who are less fortunate.

HOW GENEROUS ARE WE?

Those faithful to WAFR would interpret this story differently and use it to affirm a picture of America that is generous at its heart. That is attractive, but ultimately untrue.

Though my story might be an outlier, many of us have stories like mine, and the majority culture promotes them as possible. Stories like this get put on brochures and are material for TED Talks. The subtle testimony is that generosity in America is working, has worked in the past, and ought to work everywhere else. This narrative of relationship-based generosity is the standard belief in America, but it is not the reality by a long shot.

The lie proclaimed here is that we are the most generous nation in the world and that the more we have, the more we give. But research reveals that those are "alternative facts," also known as lies. During the Great Recession, the poorest Americans actually increased their giving while the wealthiest decreased theirs.[3]

My own life reflects this reality. Generally, the generosity of the context I grew up in was necessary because we were so dependent on others, whereas the charity that I saw among those I encountered post-college was given out of excess. When the wealthy who follow WAFR perceive a financial loss, their giving stops, but when things get tough for those on the bottom, their pockets open up. Regarding giving in America, I often hear, "Make sure you're secure, and then you can give!" Many of my college classmates proclaimed that when they make enough for themselves, they will start to give. Sadly, though, having enough never really comes, because greed is always greater than our desire to give.

When white supremacists gathered in Charlottesville in August, 2017, and a young female advocate was run over and killed by a car as they clashed with counterprotesters, the hashtag #ThisIsNotUs emerged. Charlottesville, Virginia, is perhaps more emblematic of white supremacy and wealth through the labor and sexual exploitation of African slaves and genocide of Native peoples than any other US city. Yet the resistance to confessing this reality of corporate brokenness is fierce and obstinate. The more grievous and entrenched the pattern of sin, the more vehemently we must resist to remain free in Christ. Thus the greed and self-absorption that drives the engine of America's economy needs the perception of generosity to shield our fragile culture from the truth of our corporate, exploitative selfishness.

WAFR would reframe the story of our work in northern Uganda with a focus on the vision and gifts of the people involved—not God at work. With nonprofits and donors as the idols to be imitated, we would get the glory and the American idol stays intact. Generous, successful Americans, World Vision staff, and we who served would be admired and praised. According to WAFR, the good results are just results of hard work and dedication, not a loving response to a God who loved us first.

Conversely, with Jesus of Nazareth at the center, the focus is remarkably different, and the story may or may not get reported because it is contingent on blessing others and glorifying God. The script, according to the ministry of reconciliation and the command to love the Lord our God and our neighbors as ourselves, may read like this:

> I have plans to prosper you and not to harm you, says the Lord to his people at all times. No weapon formed against you shall prosper. God Almighty hears all of those are oppressed and in need and has sent his Son to redeem and his Spirit to fill us and all the earth. The Lord God opens his hands and satisfies the needs of every living thing. And though the fig tree might not blossom and the olive fall from the tree, I and all those involved will say, bless the Lord.

This text may read as unrelated, which is understandable. These passages paraphrased from Jeremiah, Psalms, Habakkuk, and Isaiah, place our focus on God as trustworthy, our protector and provider, and as worthy of honor, attention, and glory. God is the center of the story, not us. It has been said that neither the canvas nor the brushes for a painting are famous, but instead the artist receives honor. How much more so, as God weaves our lives into this tapestry of redemption, should he receive honor and not us?

WAFR defines generosity and confers its own honor and praise on its citizen worshipers, which affirms a national generosity that is dishonest and deceptive. For example, overseas aid from the US government casts America as the savior of the world, with photos on newscasts of pallets of supplies receiving smiling faces in large crowds that eagerly receive the gifts after natural disasters. But these images should be replaced by images of crates of weapons and payouts to government soldiers and military factions where our national interests are best served. The Council on Foreign Relations notes, "There has long been broad bipartisan agreement on foreign aid on the moral and strategic significance of foreign aid. Aid levels rose sharply after the 9/11 attacks, with policymakers seeing global economic development as a way to promote U.S. national security."[4]

With only 0.1 percent of our federal budget going to foreign aid and almost 50 percent of that foreign aid going toward military and political interests, it is easy to see that the moral part of this argument is far outweighed by the strategic factors.[5] This strategic significance is further proven when we see that the top five countries that receive aid are located where the United States is fighting an enemy or supporting an ally. At 0.1 percent, the United States is ranked twentieth out of twenty-eight developed countries in foreign aid, though we have the largest economy. This makes logical sense, though, as America's values abroad are rooted in practices at home.

In America, 16 percent of federal income taxes go toward mandated national defense, and 54 percent of discretionary spending goes to the military: "The ratio of military spending to food and agriculture spending in the full budget is 4-to-1."[6] Moreover, Americans filed taxes on 10.17 trillion dollars in 2015, yet gave away 373 billion during the same time.[7] That is 3.3 percent of total earnings. To put that in perspective, the Bureau of Labor reports that the average American household spends the same amount of money on clothing as on charitable giving.

Though many Americans believe they don't have the money to give, there is a broad narrative that US citizens are generous in time and expertise as well. This is also untrue: only one in four Americans volunteer. And this number is lower in our larger cities like New York and Miami.

Similar to the US government, US citizens' time, talent, and money is oriented toward self-interest. This stark dichotomy is seen most clearly when we compare the church in Acts with followers of WAFR, including those who purport to be following Jesus. Christians today give less per capita than they did during the Great Depression; only 3 to 5 percent of Christians tithe, with most confessing Christians giving 2 to 3 percent of their income.[8] This is at or below the national average for charitable giving. Contrast this with the radical generosity of God himself and the generosity of the early church in the face of Roman oppression.

REAL GENEROSITY

Usually when American Christians think of prosperity, it is framed solely in financial and material terms. I too am guilty of using Scriptures to falsely bolster this argument. Psalm 24:1 proclaims that "The earth is the LORD's, and all it contains, / the world, and those who dwell in it," and Psalm 50:10 declares that God owns "the cattle on a thousand hills." These were some of my favorite passages to reference because I thought they were about God being my provider and giving me whatever I ask of him. This promise from Jesus to the disciples was a favorite of mine as well:

> Truly I tell you, at the renewal of all things, when the Son of Man
> sits on his glorious throne, you who have followed me will also

sit on twelve thrones, judging the twelve tribes of Israel. And everyone who has left houses or brothers or sisters or father or mother or wife or children or fields for my sake will receive a hundred times as much and will inherit eternal life. (Matthew 19:28-29 NIV)

My error was that I chose to center on my wants, needs, and plans, and I looked to God for what he had to offer me. Then I twisted the message of his words to validate that selfish narrative.

Psalm 24 is one of praise proclaiming the attributes of God, not what he will make available to me. The psalm ends with resounding exaltation, inviting us to raise our heads, open the gates, and welcome the King of glory. It does not end with instructions on how to access God's possessions. Furthermore, Psalm 50 is about God's judgment of Israel because it broke covenant with him. God's vast wealth and its coming distribution to Israel is not central here; instead, the core message is a warning of coming condemnation if the wickedness of lying, slander, and deceit continues.

The context of Matthew 19 is the parable of the rich young ruler, whose wealth stands in the way of eternal life with God—no matter his religiosity. In Matthew 19:21-22, Jesus says, "If you want to be perfect, go, sell your possessions and give to the poor, and you will have treasure in heaven. Then come, follow me.' When the young man heard this, he went away sad, because he had great wealth" (NIV).

The invaluable wealth promised in this passage is life eternal with God, and the wealth that is idolized by the young ruler is material. The ruler is bankrupt by the standards of the kingdom of God, yet rich in the eyes of the world. So, the focus here is not on the material provision of God but Christ as the true treasure.

Therefore, being truly rich means having a home in God through Christ. True generosity, then, is extending that presence to others for the flourishing of all creation. This is reflected in Paul's description of Christ's sacrifice in Philippians 2:1-11.

In this passage, we see that Jesus laid aside his privileges as the Son of God and lowered himself from the right hand of his Father to dwell among people. He entered this world not as a ruler but as a child of impoverished parents. The Son of the living God, by whom, for whom, and through whom all things were made, left his seat on the throne to give us access to all he had. In his birth, life, and ultimate death on the cross, he laid aside all wealth and position, being separated from the Father so that we might never be separated from him. Christ's loving sacrifice is an example of how we are to live (and perhaps die). He used his sinless sacrifice as a ransom for our sinfulness, performing the ultimate act of justice. Old Testament scholar Bruce Waltke defines the "just" as those who are "willing to disadvantage themselves to advantage the community."[9]

This type of sacrifice was considered foolish and confusing to those in power during the third century. This love befuddled the Alexandrians as Christians cared for those stricken with the plague. St. Dionysius the Great wrote the following:

> In their exceeding love and brotherly-kindness, they did not spare themselves, but kept by each other, and visited the sick without thought of their own peril, and ministered to them assiduously, and treated them for their healing in Christ, died from time to time most joyfully along with them, lading themselves with pains derived from others, and drawing upon themselves their neighbors' diseases, and willingly taking over to their own persons the burden of the sufferings of those around them. And many who had thus cured others of their sicknesses, and restored them to strength, died themselves, having transferred to their own bodies the death that lay upon these.[10]

This picture of mercy because of Christ was juxtaposed with those not following Jesus who treated the sick poorly. Dionysius goes on:

> But among the heathens, all was the very reverse. For they thrust aside any who began to be sick, and kept aloof even from

their dearest friends, and cast the sufferers out on the public roads half dead, and left them unburied, and treated them with utter contempt when they died, steadily avoiding any kind of communication and intercourse with death.

Common meals modeled after the Last Supper, and caring for the poor and marginalized as though they were actual brothers and sisters regardless of ethnic background, class, and heritage, exemplified the people of God. They rejected the cultural narratives of the day that centered on the worship of the empire and pleasure seeking at all costs. Acts 2 and 4 describe a framework for an alternate way of living that is rarely seen in our present day—but when it is, we, like the Romans observing the first Christians, are confounded.

ANOTHER WAY OF LIFE

I experienced similar confusion while meeting with the Bruderhof community in Harlem, New York. Clyde Thompson, a student at City College involved in the InterVarsity Christian Fellowship chapter, approached me after a talk on ethnic conciliation and justice and invited me to his home to meet with his community over dinner. I was surprised and intrigued at what I discovered. The Bruderhof comes out of the Anabaptist Christian tradition, and their founder, Eberhard Arnold, rose to prominence in post-World War I Germany.[11] Because of their strident opposition to Nazism and commitment to peacemaking, all of the Bruderhof were forced to leave Germany. They reassembled in England before planting communities around the world.

Soon after entering their brownstone in central Harlem, I felt as though I was in a world with different rules. The Bruderhof focus on two key Scripture passages that guide their lives together: Acts 2:42-45 and Acts 4:32-35. These texts came to life for me in a new way as I sat with Jessica, a young member of the Bruderhof who studied at Hunter College. I asked about her choices for a major and course of study. She told me the community paid for her education, and her professional decisions would be determined by what made the best contribution to the community. They had one bank account, which was managed by the steward. Wages earned by members went to that bank account, resources were shared as needed, and decisions were made together on how money was spent.

Though this made scriptural sense to me, it sounded crazy considering New York City and the world today. My fears kicked in immediately. *Is she okay? Was there some kind of catch? How could individuals be free to choose with so much control? How could they trust one another? What happens if someone wants to leave?* I caught myself making judgments. *Would I be willing to enter into this kind of community and do the hard work of being so intimately tied to other people because of Jesus?*

As I ventured to the basement for dinner, simply dressed men and women gathered around the table and broke into song to say grace. I can still hear the harmonies of five verses of "Amazing Grace." In the following hours of conversation and meetings, I came to deeply admire the way the Bruderhof seek to live in the world. This is a community of Christ-followers that pooled their resources to buy a home in Harlem, and sent four of its members to college, including NYU's School of Dentistry. They live as best they can in service to those around them. Trust seems to be extended across genders and generations. Along with sharing their finances, it struck me how affirming the Bruderhof were of family while making deep commitments to single people. Unwed members lived with a family and shared at least one meal per day. It is possible to value marriage and family without idolizing it!

Of course, this is no utopia. Reading the memoir of Emmy Arnold, *A Joyful Pilgrimage*, gives us a glimpse into the difficulties of having all things in common.[12] What do the Bruderhof do when there is conflict? Theft? Mistreatment? Abuse? I read the community's great testimonies of faithfulness to Jesus amid times of deep anguish and brokenness, but what stood out to me was the willingness to press into sacrificial living while surrounded by a culture that prizes independence, autonomy, and self-reliance above all else. Their generosity went beyond race, class, family, and gender to pursue the beloved community Christ calls us to on this side of heaven. These are white people by America's definition, but WAFR is not their faith.

They are not trying to build a Christian empire, but instead resist the empire of America through creating a new, different kind of family. The intent of the Bruderhof to bear witness to Jesus through a common purse is in itself a powerful testimony. There are examples of this type of radical giving rooted in the economy of Jesus among immigrant Pentecostal churches, urban Anabaptists, orders of the Catholic Church, and evangelical traditions all over the world. His kingdom is not bound by time or context, and we all have access.

The generosity of God creates access for all people as he offers himself and all that he has without cost. For followers of Jesus, God defines what it is to prosper; therefore he also determines what it is to be generous. Jesus can't be Lord and share the throne of our hearts with anything else. And it seems clear now that the heart of America is like that of the rich young ruler from Matthew 19. Jesus died for us that we might have life with him, but he also allows us to walk away.

QUESTIONS FOR INDIVIDUAL REFLECTION AND SMALL GROUP DISCUSSION

- What were your dominant feelings as you read this chapter: curiosity, hope, surprise, confusion, numbness, familiarity, distance, or something else?
- When were those feelings most present?
- What phrases, stories, or historical events resonated with you?
- What events or narratives were you unaware of? What did you learn?
- Where do you disagree or have concerns?
- What questions are you carrying?

DREAM WITH GOD

Ask a friend, a family member, or at least two other people to read through Acts 1–7 with you for seven weeks. Independently write down what practices, habits, and disciplines mark your individual and corporate walks with God. Next, write what practices, habits, and disciplines marked the walk of the early church. On your own, take time to pray and ask God which practices you should try to integrate into your own life and in your home and community.

Bring your two lists and your desired practices to your friends, family, or community and have a communal time of sharing. Without judgment or ridicule, share your conclusions with one another and commit to at least one individual and communal practice from the early church that you would like to integrate into your home context.

LIE 9

AMERICA IS THE LAND OF THE FREE

WHITNEY HOUSTON'S RENDITION of the national anthem at the 1991 Super Bowl was powerful. The stadium roared as Houston held on to the final note with her arms fully extended. This ballad of white American folk religion, complete with an F-16 flyover, is an assertion of the reality and the aspiration that American is the "land of the free." Sadly, the claim and hope of true freedom in WAFR is as reliable as a barrel without a bottom.

Life in America is much more like our public perception of Flint, Michigan, than the private story we tell ourselves of life in the Hamptons or the Upper East Side of Manhattan. Material poverty, contaminated water and air, and devastating segregation are less apparent in Long Island and New York City, but the same suffering is just as present in those places as in their Great Lakes counterpart. This is true of every revered and reviled town and city. Whether in the great outdoors with no neighbors for miles, the cul-de-sacs of the suburbs, or fast-paced urban centers, there are degrees of brokenness. Nowhere is brokenness absent. But this truth is hidden behind the WAFR claim that material wealth and power yield joy and happiness. There is no freedom in fantasy, only a different type of imprisonment. Because the American dream never delivers what it promises, followers of WAFR become slaves to the lives we believe we deserve, have earned, or are working for. Claiming to be free while following WAFR is denial; and a confession of enslavement to ambition, material wealth, pleasure, and comfort—which is no freedom at all.

SEARCHING FOR FREEDOM

I vividly remember believing I was somewhere different in December 2005. I was a sophomore at Columbia University, active on campus and in Christian ministry. I was finishing my second book and talking with publishers while also performing spoken-word poetry off-campus. From the outside, things were going well. Beneath the surface, though, I was desperate to find myself and a place in this city as a person, not just a performer. To help pay for the publication of *The Second Verse*, I took a job as a real estate agent for Prudential Douglas-Elliman. The day of my interview, the workers who operated the subway system went on strike. Since I didn't have money for a taxi, I walked the hundred blocks to my interview. That made an impression on the broker, and I got the job. A month later I passed the exam and was part of the Real Estate Board of New York. I thought to myself, *This is how you "make it," right?* I was studying by day, composing poetry whenever I had a free moment, and working a job to finance the dream. I thought I was free.

No one knew my suits were from the Goodwill or that I wore the same shirt over and over. Clients rarely thought I was an undergraduate and respected my quick wit and knowledge about the market. The ruse that I created wasn't working only on others but also on me. That was . . . until it didn't anymore.

A few weeks into the job I was standing next to my white boss in the heart of Harlem on the corner of 125th and Lennox, both of us armed with our suits, smartphones, and Starbucks. An older African American male looked at me, looked at my boss, shook his head, and walked away. I know this look. This is a look of disapproval. I saw this look from black women when my white female high school friends got out of my truck. I saw this look when I walked with my classmates from Columbia to the closest KFC. This is a look of "You must be an Uncle Tom, a house n——, a sellout." And all of a sudden, I was just a nineteen-year-old black male who wasn't free from anything and still wasn't comfortable in my own skin. But then the traffic signal changed and we crossed the street onto the next block, going to another open house. I took those feelings of hurt, sadness, and lost-ness, and stuffed them—until they surfaced again.

My boss hired another African American man, not to work in the office but instead in a brownstone that he owned in need of renovation. The man's job was to clean it out. There were dust masks, garbage bags, and a huge orange garbage container out in the street. The stage was set for him to get to work, and work he did—but I'm not sure how much he got paid. He showed up angry at our office one day and shouted (among many things): "You don't know me, Rob! You think you know me?" And before storming out, he said, "I'll tear this place apart." Again, I felt the familiar tug to speak up for the person who looked like me, not the boss who didn't. Yet I said nothing as this man from Harlem looked at me and stomped to the elevator. The inevitable happened shortly thereafter. Within the week I found myself out of a suit and in a work setting more similar to how I grew up. I put on those work gloves, that dust mask, and filled the trash can with the guts of my boss's brownstone.

This work wasn't beneath who I was in Brodnax, but I was conflicted to be doing it in New York. *I didn't come here to do construction*, I told myself. I pondered, *What will people think of me on the other side of Morningside Park when I walk back up those steps smelling like manual labor and dressed like this? Would anyone believe I was a Columbia student?*

I consistently felt more out of place as weekend open houses replaced Sunday morning church services, and midweek Bible studies were crowded out by poetry and homework. That was until one weekend it snowed, and I secretly hoped that the open houses on the schedule would be canceled. I took off the $20 suit I had on and got excited about going to church with my best friend. Then I got the phone call that the open houses were happening. The suit went back on and I started the forty-five-minute walk to East Harlem in the snow. I got there and no one came. For two hours I sat in a million-dollar apartment, and then I spent another two hours in a million-dollar brownstone with Ella Fitzgerald's "Take the 'A' Train" playing in the background at both locations. I was frustrated and sad—but not desperate enough to quit.

No one was coming to these open houses, and while in the office that following Saturday I called my boss and suggested that we cancel the Sunday showings. Another storm was coming, so I thought we should take the day off. He responded by raising his voice, and I don't respond well to being yelled at. He yelled at me the way I had seen him yell at others. I didn't respond in a professional manner, but it changed his tone. I don't remember what else was said, and the phone call ended abruptly.

After hanging up the phone, I said out loud, "Why don't I feel like I belong here?"

And a voice responded, "Because you don't."

There was no one else in the office. I got up and checked all the cubicles around me. There was no one there. I spent the afternoon praying and thinking about why I took this job in the first place. The only reason was money.

GOD AS PROVIDER

The prevailing lie that I believed about God was that he wouldn't provide for me so I needed to provide for myself. I believed I had to make the first move and meet God halfway even though that is nowhere in Scripture or modeled by Jesus.

I asked God for forgiveness for trusting myself not him, and as a sign of that trust I submitted my two weeks' notice.

That was the first time that God spoke to me audibly and I obeyed. Sadly, it didn't take long for me to find another financial carrot to follow in the effort to provide for myself. This time, a start-up magazine was the temptation. It came with an apartment for the summer, four thousand dollars a month, and the chance to build a brand leveraging all of my gifts to empower young people. I didn't pray, read the Bible, or in any way check with God to see if this was from him. After all, the CEO was a US Army veteran from Barbados who seemed to want the best for the world around him. I thought that with the money, housing, and mission, it had to be. So, I went all in.

This time I didn't buy two-dollar suit jackets; instead I went on a shopping spree with my first paycheck. I paid some overdue bills for my mom and took that Macy's credit card discount because I thought I would be a regular shopper. This is the blessed life that pastors talk about, right?

Two weeks after signing on the dotted line, the situation began to unravel.

I thought about my life as I drove ten hours back home for the funeral of my elderly cousin, Ms. Olive. She had acted as a grandmother for two generations on Allen Road where I grew up. She was a regal woman who never lost her quality. At her funeral, I was confronted with the gospel of Jesus, which was in stark contrast to my gospel of greed. Feeling convicted as I headed back to NYC, I again resolved that I would live differently. But of course, I would keep my job, clothes, and apartment.

At that time my understanding of following Jesus meant I did not have to give those things up. In fact, that would be foolish. I didn't merely believe that hard work, money, and accomplishments could insulate me from suffering; I was a disciple and an evangelist of that idea. The fact that I couldn't free myself from pain through hard work and that Jesus was the original abolitionist, able to free me from physical and spiritual chains, was overwhelming. I was quickly overtaken by the view of the skyline, the pace of the F-train, and the lack of money in my account.

The reality of my limits struck more fully when I reached my summer apartment to find it had been repossessed. Confused, I called my boss and discovered that he hadn't paid the rent there for months. The landlord was not sympathetic to my cause because he didn't know who I was or that I was living there. I ventured to Columbia University with the clothes on my back. Fortunately, summer housing was available and there was a dorm room that I could stay in. Grateful, I decided to put down my things, find some food and, honestly, some clean underwear. Going to the ATM to grab cash, I discovered that not only had my boss not paid the landlord, but he hadn't paid me either. My paycheck had bounced, and I was firmly in the negative. I went back to my room and cried. I was incensed. I took this man at his word, paid bills for my mom, and invested my time and reputation to make this venture a success—for what? I would like to say that the next thing I did was pray or lean into Christian community, but it wasn't.

TO BE SET FREE

Instead of nurturing my relationship with God during my time at Columbia, I medicated my loneliness and frustrations with food, porn, and working out. Overeating, masturbation, and the gym were my comfort instead of the presence of God. I had no money and food was out of reach, but I had my computer, so porn was readily accessible. It didn't bring Ms. Olive back, unlock that apartment door, pay my mom's bills, or hug me. The only thing that self-gratification did was deepen my addiction and cause me to objectify women. And after realizing again that an orgasm fixed nothing, I asked God to help me. And he did—my computer stopped working. The thing that I was using to access my idol wouldn't turn on.

I called Ashley Byrd, my InterVarsity staff worker, and told him all that happened. As we sat on a bench near the entrance to Morningside Park, my true longings came out. With his probing questions, I blurted out, "Why do you care about me?" Why would an ex-wrestler from Hawaii be sitting in a park in Harlem at night with a black man from Brodnax? He responded that it's what Jesus had done for him. And all of a sudden, the Jesus that people talked about became real. I moved from being a believer to a disciple. I moved from trying to think the right way and do whatever I wanted to being a child of God and living as though I am in the family of Christ.

That day I moved from being an enemy of God to a friend of the King. This was true freedom, and I tasted it. It was not the freedom that Whitney Houston sang about or etched in the US Constitution. It was freedom that didn't require my effort, investment, or anything else. All it "required" was that I receive it, which turned out to be the hardest thing for me to do. Freedom isn't free, as the saying goes, but the gospel of Jesus Christ says that Jesus paid the price for us.

I am firmly convinced that this truth sets us free—Jesus sets us free from the laws of sin and death, and therefore no freedom exists outside of a relationship with God through Christ. Every other freedom is false; to claim otherwise is a lie. My contention is that the leader of the free world is Jesus, though American citizens regularly claim that the president is the "leader of the free world." America's commander-in-chief leads an army that seeks to bring freedom to others through donation, diplomacy, or destruction. Yet, these practices only set those involved free to be bound to something else that suits American interests.

Therefore, my father and others who went to Vietnam were not spreading true freedom, but instead were trying to bring submission to an American idea of liberty. My cousin and childhood friends who served in Baghdad and Afghanistan and have PTSD don't look free, and neither do those they fought for here or abroad. Yet, that is the freedom offered by WAFR, and it is far from the freedom we find Christ.

DONALD RUMSFELD, A HOTEL IN SEOUL, AND WHITE AMERICAN FOLK RELIGION

This difference is seen not only in the founding documents of the United States. It also has been freshly articulated in recent history. On March 19, 2004, the one-year anniversary of Operation Iraqi Freedom, Donald Rumsfeld, the US secretary of defense from 2001 to 2006 under President George W. Bush, published an article titled "The Price of Freedom" in the *New York Times*. The previous March the United States invaded Iraq to remove Saddam Hussein, to supposedly prevent the proliferation of weapons of mass destruction and prevent another 9/11-like terrorist attack. These weapons were never discovered and the Iraqi government played no role in the attacks of September 11, 2001, that destroyed the Twin Towers, damaged the Pentagon, and downed Flight 93 over Pennsylvania.

A South Korean journalist asked Rumsfeld why her fellow citizens should join the United States in Iraq. He quipped that a similar question could have been asked of Americans decades before. He then recounts,

> I asked the woman to look out the window—at the lights, the cars, the energy of the vibrant economy of South Korea. I told her about a satellite photo of the Korean peninsula, taken at night, that I keep on a table in my Pentagon office. North of the demilitarized zone there is nothing but darkness—except a pin-prick of light around Pyongyang—while the entire country of South Korea is ablaze in light, the light of freedom.[1]

Rumsfeld linked the sacrifice of American lives to the life, liberty, and happiness that South Koreans presently enjoy. The sacrifice of Americans afforded South Korea the opportunity to bask in "the light of freedom." He failed to mention that the Korean War took place in the 1950s when the United States' government and its citizens perpetrated violent abuses against communities of color, including mass deportations of immigrants to Mexico, the reign of Jim Crow laws in the South, and the reintegration of Japanese Americans into their communities after their unjust internment.[2] Freedom, as articulated by Rumsfeld in keeping with the founders of the United States, has little to do with the flourishing of all people—who are made in the image of God—and the abundant life made available through Christ. Instead, it has everything to do with creating the best path for those who are deemed worthy of pursuing wealth and self-determined happiness as well as its deference and maintenance.

The vision Rumsfeld cast was not one free of racism, discrimination, and hatred, but one of "lights, the cars, the energy of the vibrant economy." The freedom he desired to spread to Iraq from South Korea was the freedom to worship at the altar of performance and worth based on economic output and comfort. He wanted to spread WAFR so the god of prosperity could bless those who merit it and condemn those who don't. In the story, Rumsfeld dehumanized Saddam Hussein; WAFR is not meant for him. This dehumanization justifies the use of violence against him, his family, and the Iraqi forces who would later become a significant portion of the Islamic State.[3]

> In Iraq, for 12 years, through 17 United Nations Security Council resolutions, the world gave Saddam Hussein every opportunity to avoid war. He was being held to a simple standard: live up to your agreement at the end of the 1991 Persian Gulf War; disarm and prove you have done so. Instead of disarming—as Kazakhstan, South Africa, and Ukraine did, and as Libya is doing today—Saddam Hussein chose deception and defiance.[4]

Rumsfeld went on to frame Hussein as disobedient to international norms, especially highlighting the ways the Iraqi military attacked neighboring countries. Rumsfeld argued that it was not America's desire to fight, but its duty to spread "self-governance" to the people of Iraq. Hussein brought this upon himself, and according to Rumsfeld, historians would judge this war to be a just conflict, just as in Germany, Italy, Japan, and Korea. He then explained not only the economic benefits to Iraq but also the rights now granted to Iraqis through the interim constitution that is very similar to America's founding documents:

> It guarantees freedom of religion and expression; the right to assemble and to organize political parties; the right to vote; and the right to a fair, speedy and open trial. It prohibits discrimination based on gender, nationality and religion, as well as arbitrary arrest and detention. A year ago, today, none of those protections could have been even imagined by the Iraqi people.[5]

Again, Rumsfeld makes no mention of the unfair trials, voter suppression, racism, and hate crimes in the United States occurring at the times this article was published. True to WAFR's willingness to forgo details detrimental to its goals and point toward a future that preserves itself, Rumsfeld closed with an invitation to express appreciation to American military service members who fight for freedom around the world.

Rumsfeld's opinion piece summarized what American freedom is; it is an up-to-date rendition of "life, liberty, and the pursuit of happiness." In WAFR, we are made to want cars, lights, restaurants, and economic growth and opportunity. And the price of this freedom is the lives, minds, limbs, and livelihoods of men and women in every country involved. In the eyes of Rumsfeld and those in power this is good and necessary, and should be praised and appreciated. Opinion pieces like this are meant to galvanize, inspire, and invite. Rumsfeld implies that this South Korean journalist, the South Korean people, and any reader of this piece should join this movement without question or hesitation. The invitation from Jesus is different.

FREEDOM IN CHRIST

True freedom is found in the kingdom of God. It is articulated well in John 8:31-47. In it we see another confrontation between Jesus and the religious leaders of his day, the Pharisees. Prior to this encounter Jesus prevented the stoning of an adulterous woman and claimed he was the light of the world. Now, he challenged their paradigms of freedom and identity. True freedom in this passage is found in the life, death, and resurrection of Jesus. It is not the freedom available in the proper limitation of government, which the US founding fathers falsely say is the essence of freedom. Jesus offers us freedom from punishment for opposing God's purposes in the world. There is freedom from the debilitating effects of present and eternal wrongs committed by us against us and other people. The freedom that Jesus offers is admission into the presence of God via a relationship with the resurrected Son.

The Pharisees did not understand this at first, and the more they did, the more they didn't like it. The slavery they perceived was literal, and the lineage they claimed was focused on bloodline. Jesus was pointing beyond Abraham toward the God who promised descendants to Abraham and Sarah. The Pharisees were further confused by this pushback, and Jesus says they are descendants of the devil. Jesus proclaims that he is telling the truth because he is the Son of God, the author of all truth. Furthermore, anyone who believes he is not who he claims to be is a liar and son of the Father of Lies. Therefore, to call Jesus a liar is to align with the devil and claim a seat at the table of the enemy.

In John 8:48-59 the Jewish leaders responded to Jesus' teaching with a racial slur—"you are a Samaritan"—and accused him of being possessed by a demon. In context, Samaritans were of Canaanite and Hebrew descent. These two groups hated and were often violent toward one another. That along with the suggestion that Jesus was actually an instrument of Satan reveals the level of intensity in this interaction. Jesus did not back down. He asserted his place and identity within the historical and present while making clear his judgment against them. Their response was to try to kill Jesus. But he escaped while they were picking up stones to throw at him.

The truth that Jesus spoke and embodied upended the rules of that time and continues to do the same in our present day. Traditional American conservatives tend to define freedom in economic terms, with free markets and economies measured by economic growth, personal wealth, and individual liberty. And traditionally politically liberal Americans generally tend to define freedom in terms of social and environmental justice, sexual liberation, reproductive freedom, free expression, and a higher level of government involvement. Jesus transcends both of these perspectives and defines freedom in spiritual terms as liberation from sin and the restoration of shalom. This spiritual transformation has material effects as spiritual shalom leads to concrete steps toward social and economic freedom for those around followers of Jesus.

Sitting on that park bench and looking out into the New York City night, I had to choose between the freedom offered to me by my present circumstance in America or the freedom extended to me by Jesus. One version of that freedom, per Donald Rumsfeld, was obtained through human effort by using might, skill, and intellect to gain and guard what I have earned. The other would require trust in Jesus, obedience to his will, and suspension of effort to attain perfection for myself.

Freedom in the world includes a kingdom riddled with addiction, abuse, exploitation, and violence. Freedom in Christ comes from embracing the presence of the living God, where there is perfect peace. Rumsfeld invited the Korean people to fight and die for the freedom of the Iraqis, just as America fought and died for Koreans. Jesus died so I wouldn't have to.

Rumsfeld's argument was much like that of the men who arrived on the shores of countries yet to be colonized. They offered a truncated gospel, a cherry-picked Bible, and money to the natives if they were willing to work or barter with the pale-faced men. And the reality is that an invitation to work without certain payment or reward is dishonest at best and slavery at worst. The truth is that an invitation to pursue life, liberty, and happiness, as defined by those who are willing to lie, cheat, steal, and kill to implement their system of government, is not freedom but exploitative oppression. Jesus, on the other hand, pays the price for our freedom and gives his life in exchange for ours, requiring nothing in return for his sacrifice. We can opt into the household of faith or remain outside of it.

Jesus' invitation to me was not to enlist in a nation's army but into the family of God. I had the choice to say yes or no, and I was loved independent of my desire to give that love in return. All I needed to do was accept and embrace that he alone could free me. In Christ alone I find my freedom. I stand today on this truth, and it has made me free. It set me free from addiction, self-hatred, a destructive view of those with differing opinions, and an oppressive view of women. Moreover, this truth freed me from workaholism and an identity rooted in my accomplishments, ushering me into an abundance not defined by the forefathers of this nation but by my Father in heaven. The truth in Romans 5:8 that "while we were yet sinners, Christ died for us" grounds my seeking of love and justice for all people, including those who would see me as less than human because of the color of my skin. In Christ, I am not working to be free; I live out of the freedom I've received.

Not only does WAFR define freedom differently from the God of the Bible, it offers no freedom at all. Jesus offers true freedom to all people. He shines a light on the invisible prisons of the one in eight people in the United States who abuse alcohol and the one in three men and women who experience sexual and physical violence. Jesus died to free the twenty US military veterans who commit suicide every day and he rose from the dead for the 50 percent of the America children who live at or near poverty.[6] He gave his life to guarantee our freedom, not a job we have to work for.

QUESTIONS FOR INDIVIDUAL REFLECTION AND SMALL GROUP DISCUSSION

- What were your dominant feelings as you read this chapter: curiosity, hope, surprise, confusion, numbness, familiarity, distance, or something else?

- When were those feelings most present?

- What phrases, stories, or historical events resonated with you?

- What events or narratives were you unaware of? What did you learn?

- Where do you disagree or have concerns?

- What questions are you carrying?

WALKING IN THE FREEDOM JESUS OFFERS, NOT THE FREEDOM OF THE WORLD

Our world is increasingly marked by loneliness, anxiety, fear, apathy, and cynicism. Jesus offers freedom from all of that through his love and his offer of abundant life. This freedom empowers us to engage deeply with the world around us, being fully present to joy and suffering, pain and delight.

- Where do you desire to see freedom in your own life? How about the lives of those around you?

- In those places where you desire freedom, what actions and habits have you or others used to seek freedom apart from Jesus?

- What concrete disciplines of prayer and engagement with Scripture could you use to receive your freedom through Jesus, not through your own efforts and solutions?

- What do you need from Jesus and the community around you to help you live in the reality of the freedom Christ has paid for us?

- Which of the steps above could you invite your family and friends to do alongside you?

LIE 10

AMERICA IS THE HOME OF THE BRAVE

"DO YOU HAVE A SHOTGUN?"

That's what well-meaning American men of every ethnicity ask me in jest when I express fear about my daughter becoming a teenager. This picture of a father in an undershirt with or without a gun chasing a boy out of his daughter's bedroom, the backseat of a car, or the last row in a movie theater is supposed to communicate protection, safety, and care. The 2008 movie *Taken* is the extreme depiction of this reality. In it Liam Neeson's character says this to a sex trafficker who kidnapped his daughter:

> I don't know who you are. I don't know what you want. If you're looking for ransom, I can tell you I don't have money. But what I do have is a very particular set of skills—skills I have acquired over a very long career. Skills that make me a nightmare for people like you. If you let my daughter go now, that will be the end of it. I will not look for you. I will not pursue you. But if you don't, I will look for you. I will find you, and I will kill you.[1]

The voice on the other end of the phone replies, "Good luck." This sets off a series of events that includes this papa bear shooting a corrupt police officer's wife in front of their kids, torturing criminals for information, and wounding and killing many people. This is all in the name of liberating his daughter from those who pay to rape women and those who profit from sexual exploitation. Simply put, these special skills plus the love for his daughter equal the dismantling of a human trafficking ring and his daughter coming home. This father is deemed brave and courageous, and he became the paradigm for many young, passionate advocates who approached me at events about ending modern-day slavery. The men who watched this film downloaded the same message I did from society. The peak of bravery and courage is my ability and willingness to violently defend women. This courage and bravery multiply when men are willing to use violence and even die to protect those we deem innocent and vulnerable.

As a new abolitionist working with leaders interested in ending modern-day slavery, I spent many hours correcting this attitude in those who desired to end labor and sexual exploitation by violent means, not knowing that this same lie was rooted deeply within me.[2] I say this because in response to many of the men who asked whether I had a shotgun, I replied, "No, I don't need one," presenting my closed fists. I was glad to affirm my willingness to participate in socially acceptable violence. These were symptoms of a deeper insecurity I had about my ability to protect my daughter from the tragedy of sexual violence and my lack of faith that Christ would be with her in every circumstance.

FEAR COMES FROM LACK OF FAITH

In his book *The Deeper Journey*, Robert Mulholland shares that individuals who create and project a false self must build defenses to justify and protect that perception. For example, if I want to present myself as wealthy, successful, and put together, my social media feed reflects this reality. Photos of my beautiful partner on vacation in an exotic location or a hole-in-the-wall restaurant that is yet to be discovered fill my social media profiles. I may put up photos of my latest purchases or ask for advice on the next expensive gadget I desire, not because I am looking for knowledge from the community, but because I want the community to know I'm thinking about these things.

Therefore my wife and friends, along with the material things I purchase, become tools to hold together a façade I present to the world. This false projection of myself becomes my identity. Consequently, when the things that make up my identity are threatened, I must defend them because they are essential to my false self.

So, practically speaking, when I think about my daughter growing into a young woman, I am filled with anxiety that is difficult to articulate. I know she will be sexualized by society. And the profit made by the *Taken* film franchise and TV program verify that this fear is not unique to me.

I know that I can't be with her at all times or protect her from every man or woman that she walks past. But to admit my fear and inability to guide and control every situation in my daughter's life is paralyzing. So I hide behind threats about what I could do with my fists, feet, and a knife or firearm.

I must admit I feel the same about my wife and other women around me. There is so little that I can influence or control. This fear is not driven by ISIS or international terror groups but by the reality of being a woman of color in a country that doesn't hold men or women in power accountable or protect victims of sexual violence. This is not the fear of foreign invasion or a missile strike but of abuse and violence from the police or people in our pulpits, congregations, and neighborhoods. Thus, to feel powerful and brave I want to arm my wife, daughter, and myself with some socially acceptable protections, and violence is just fine. This is not a coincidence—it's ingrained within WAFR.

The unwavering invitation from WAFR is to pursue life, liberty, and happiness at all costs, and that includes the covert and overt actions taken to protect this way of life. Actors like Liam Neeson embody this as their fists, feet, and bullets hurt people for a seemingly just cause. The higher the level of comfort, stability, and security of my loved ones (and me), the higher my worth must be.

This builds my false self: a social tower of babel that is a reflection of my own greatness in the world. Therefore, anything that threatens life, liberty, and the pursuit of happiness must be removed. Contrary to the biblical narrative, instead of being married and a father by God's grace, these blessings are somehow linked to my hard work and personal awesomeness.

This wrong thinking means that my daughter, my wife, and all those I care for are not gifts from God made in his image, but possessions that reflect *me* wherever they go. And to protect my image, I must protect them. And I must protect them not because I am loving, brave, and courageous but because I am afraid. I am afraid that if they are violated it will reflect poorly on me. So to save face, I say I'm saving them. And WAFR bids me to do the same for the United States. There are certainly holy motivators for protecting one's family, but those were not at work in my case.

As Puritan leader and future governor of Massachusetts John Winthrop said circa 1630, "[We] are a city on a hill," linking this new country to Jesus' Sermon on the Mount (Matthew 5).[3] That would become the United States' supposed covenant with God to be his beacon of freedom, prosperity, democracy, and a place where all people can achieve their economic potential. And thus, with a God-ordained destiny to fulfill, citizens must at all costs fight to protect their peace, prosperity, and freedom as defined by the framers of this nation. This "Christian" white nationalism is un-Christian, unbiblical, and antithetical to the Jesus of Scripture but core to WAFR. This belief and its practices are toxic, tragic, and unfortunately still in operation today. There is no other place where this lie about bravery and its link to violence is more destructive than in the treatment of American military service members, law enforcement officers, their families, and those who engage in this false bravery and the praise they receive for it from nearby and worldwide.

One Thanksgiving I asked my father why he went to Vietnam. He began by describing the segregation that existed in Prince Edward County, where he grew up. Farmville is famous for its role in providing plaintiffs for *Brown v. the Board of Education*. This landmark decision made it illegal to segregate American schools based on skin color. But just because something is illegal doesn't mean it doesn't continue. Thus, at nine years old my dad became part of what is known as "The Lost Generation," losing five years of his education to white leaders who refused to integrate schools. Instead they rerouted public funds to start private schools for white children, which exist to this day. This is chronicled in the Robert Russa Moton High School Building, now a national landmark and museum dedicated to studying civil rights and education.[4]

My dad went into the military due to the poverty of opportunity, community, and the systemic racism that crushed his spirit and separated his siblings. It looks like his military service was compelled less by bravery and more by desperation. Nevertheless, he explained that he wished that he had become an officer, but that would have meant another tour in Vietnam. My aunt Rebecca said to him at the prospect of another trip overseas, "If you go to a well ninety-nine times and nothing happens, you may not want to go again" meaning that if he went back to Vietnam he could be killed. He did not return.

On his face though, I could see that he wondered, *But what if?* "I wonder what it's like to walk into a room as a four-star general," he said, sitting up a little straighter.

I was silent in response but thought to myself, *I imagine it's the opposite of what happened when he tried to walk to school six decades ago.* The same man that heard "thank you for your service" as he received a free cup of coffee at McDonald's was just a grown-up boy looking for significance and acknowledgment of his humanity, experience, and potential. As I sat in the passenger side of his car two hours later listening to the words of "Nearer, My God, to Thee" as sung by the Soul Stirrers, he said, "That explains it all."[5]

The words of this old gospel song gave voice to a life punctuated by suffering and a search for purpose, identity, and enduring peace. This song's expression of faith and emotion gave him strength for the journey. This is a journey that all of us are on, hoping to reach the same destination though we are headed in different directions. My father, who is still wandering, closed his eyes under the brim of his VFW cap and nodded his head to the music.

SEARCHING FOR PURPOSE AND PEACE

Material poverty, lack of opportunity, and systemic racism may not be the leading motivations for joining the military today, but minorities, women, and impoverished regions of America are targets for recruitment and bear the human cost of war disproportionately when compared to urban, wealthier areas.[6] It's unlikely, though, that demographics and socioeconomics are the ultimate drivers for enlistment, especially as half of all recruits today are from households with incomes of $50,000 or more in America.[7] So, the true bait before my father was the same that led me to the USS Intrepid recruitment station while contemplating my own future. "The Few, the Proud, the Brave" spoke to something within me too.

I remember feeling respected when I told people where I was going to interview. I was treated like I was important in front of the recruiter. It felt good to be seen as having the potential to be an officer or even a pilot. I felt affirmed being perceived as someone who was unafraid of danger as opposed to someone who could be dangerous. Perhaps my dad felt the same the first time he put on a uniform and walked onto a ship or looked down on the land of Jim Crow from a transport plane.

The wake-up call came for me, though, when I realized that my bravery and valor would be joined with my ability and willingness to commit acts of violence in obedience to my commanding officers in the name of the values and priorities of the US government. This bravery may include the ultimate sacrifice of my life for the government-determined greater good of the American people. This is strikingly similar to how the God of Abraham, Isaac, and Jacob depicts bravery in the book of Joshua and how Paul describes Jesus in Philippians 2.

PICTURES OF BRAVERY AND COURAGE

God made God-size promises to Joshua in Joshua 1:1-9. Most notably, God laid out what it would be mean for Joshua to be bold and brave. Then, because of his obedient faithfulness to the promises of God, he was promised victory and land for the Israelites. He need only trust God and do the things God commanded, and just as God was with Moses, he would be with Joshua.

Moses heard from God and walked closely with the Lord. He spent extraordinary amounts of time with Joshua, and it's likely his death left a void in Joshua's life. Deuteronomy 34:8 says that Israel mourned for thirty days upon the death of Moses. But in keeping with what Joshua was commanded, he began to lead the Israelites on the next stage of this journey. We witness Joshua's courage, not necessarily by leading the Israelites into battle and victory but by obeying God and receiving victory through God's provision.

This is clear as Joshua took the city of Jericho. Instead of devising plans to breach Jericho's famous walls, Joshua sought the Lord, and the walls fell because of his obedience to God:

> So the people shouted, and *priests* blew the trumpets; and when the people heard the sound of the trumpet, the people shouted with a great shout and the wall fell down flat, so that the people went up into the city, every man straight ahead, and they took the city (Joshua 6:20)

This was not a victory centered on the military might of Israel but on reverence for the living God. This is made clear when juxtaposed with what happened when the Israelites attempted to take the city of Ai (Joshua 7). They were soundly defeated after scouting the land, not because of their inability to fight but because of their sin and disobedience. God responds to Joshua's prayers and lament for the thirty-six men that were killed, explaining that Israel has sinned against God, violated the covenant, and must repent or continue to fight in vain without the presence of God (Joshua 7:11-13).

Later we read that Achan had stolen a mantle, silver, and gold from Ai and buried them near his tent. This was in direct disobedience to Joshua who gave the commands from God for how Jericho was to be taken, along with a warning if they disobeyed (Joshua 7:18-19). Achan was in the crowd when Joshua confronted him. He was not ignorant of his disobedience but confessed his sin to Joshua and those assembled (Joshua 7:20-21).

After this confession and punishment, God confirmed that Joshua and the Israelites were ready to take Ai. In their obedience to God the Israelites were victorious against the Amorites. Because Joshua was leading a military conquest, it is easy to conflate his bravery with violence, yet that it not the focus of the passage. The eternal message from Joshua that endures to this day is the importance of obedience to God above all, even when it is costly and difficult.

In historical context, the Israelites practiced obedience by being in lockstep with God as they stayed behind his cloud during the day and behind his fire at the night as they wandered in the desert (Exodus 13:21). And their obedience continued after the destruction of Ai because Joshua and the people did not build an altar for him or a structure bearing his name. Instead, they gave glory, honor, and focus to God and his precepts (Joshua 8:30-35).

Their victory is a testament to the faithfulness of God and his trustworthiness to fulfill his promises, not the military leadership of Joshua. Thus, Joshua is not remembered for his bravery, but for his obedience in faith to God the Father (Hebrews 11:30).

This mirrors Paul's description of Christ in Philippians 2:1-11. Just as Joshua was called to obedience, so was Christ. Jesus didn't simply lay down his life but was sent by the Father as an atonement for our sin and to reconcile all of creation to God. This obedience to God the Father out of loving reverence is the definition of courage and a picture of bravery in Scripture. Accordingly, to be bold and courageous is not to act in individual or collective self-interest, but to love sacrificially, even and especially toward those who wish to harm us or those we care about. Moreover, to be bold and courageous is to turn away from the sin of pride that places our goals, views, and desires above those of God.

This is the bravery that stands in stark contrast to the bravery of WAFR. It is impossible to obey the King of the universe *and* the commander-in-chief of the US military in situations that place the Constitution in conflict with Holy Scripture. It is impossible for me to claim full trust and reliance on God as my refuge and strong tower while arming myself to keep all I have safe. WAFR commands me to preserve myself, my country, and our way of life. Conversely, Jesus says that whoever tries to keep their life will lose it (Luke 17:33). We can take pride in our country and the kingdom, but our allegiance cannot be to both. The two are not one and the same. My identity can't be rooted in earthly authority and founded by God at the same time.

Jesus said, "No one can serve two masters" (Matthew 6:24). This is in line with the first commandment, where God decrees, "You shall have no other gods before Me" (Exodus 20:3). We see this in the life of Daniel, who was trafficked from his home along with Shadrach, Meshach, and Abednego, and forced to assimilate into the Babylonian culture. He did nothing disrespectful and didn't harm those who harmed him. But when Daniel was told to bow down to an idol, he did not bend his knee. Similarly, though Esther was kidnapped and sexually exploited by King Xerxes, she advocated for her people yet still yielded to the authority of Yahweh and challenged the patterns of her captors. Her resistance was in response to God's beckoning, not her own fear, pain, or anger. This is also true of Nehemiah, Joseph, and many other biblical characters who chose obedience to God and disobedience to the status quo.

These passages came to life for me when I sat with a childhood friend whose husband had slept with his coworker. Her pain was palpable. Betrayal hung in the air like an invisible fog that clouded my judgment and perception of goodness. As she shared her story, I was incensed. I literally had to walk away. She expressed that she was afraid to tell me because of what I might do. Her hesitation was correct. I had no godly thoughts in mind. Here was my opportunity to be violent, and I wanted to take it. I felt completely justified in shattering her husband's nose. My plan was to invite him to our home and, before he crossed the threshold of our door, I would punch him in the face.

But revenge was not in her heart. This woman did not want me to fight her husband but to fight for her marriage through prayer and by being present with them. Before I was able to promise that, I had to sit in the presence of God.

WHAT DO BRAVERY AND COURAGE LOOK LIKE?

While reflecting, I was reminded of a man who confessed to me that he visits brothels while a young man in Fuzhou, China. He wept as he said that the last time he was there, the teenage girl that he just paid to rape looked at him and said, "Please don't ever do this again." He put on his pants and left feeling disgusted with himself. I imagined this moment a hundred times before. Prior to this, I envisioned myself putting someone like him in his place verbally and physically. He should feel some sense of the pain that he inflicted. And I get to be the one to do it. Right?

Wrong. The gospel of Christ compelled me to do otherwise.

The same is true of a young man who approached me after an event about sex trafficking. His father was a pimp, and his earliest sexual encounters had been with the women his dad claimed as property. He had even gone to a strip club the night before and recruited a young woman who was ready to sell herself for him. "It's all I know how to do," he said with his head down, awaiting something other than the embrace of God I gave to him. Both of these men, after hearing of the radical, compassionate love of Jesus and my own story of redeemed sexuality, desired to be set free and transformed.

While with these three people, I had to lay down my version of courage and WAFR's vision of bravery. Life is not an action flick, and I am not Liam Neeson but instead I'm a follower of Jesus living as a citizen of a different kingdom. So, the first time I met my friend's unfaithful husband, I had to hug him. And to this day, in private I pray for him to be led out of temptation and into a life with Jesus. I also ask God to give me a heart to move toward and not away from him, conscious of the fact I too am a sinner saved by grace.

Similarly, I did not chastise or humiliate the young student from Fuzhou. I did not leverage my community and government connections to find the fourteen-year-old girl he exploited and put him in prison in his own country. I wept with him, prayed with him, and welcomed him into the family of God the same way Ashley Byrd welcomed me when I wanted out of my addiction to porn and sexual exploitation to follow Jesus. I suggested a plan for him that included community, accountability, and a calling not to attempt to rid himself of guilt and shame but to accept the freedom afforded to him by Jesus.

I invited that son of a pimp to become the Son of the original abolitionist, the author of freedom, and to join the household under Christ. Instead of hitting him, I hugged him. Since "there is now no condemnation for those who are in Christ Jesus" (Romans 8:1), he would not receive condemnation from me.

WAFR commands that I give these men *what's coming to them* and repay them at least equal the evil that they have done; Jesus commands the opposite. Obedience to the "prince of the power of the air" (Ephesians 2:2), and in keeping with the spirit of the age, would mean violence, retaliation, social rejection, and indefinite restitution. In keeping with Liam Neeson's *Taken* character and the psyche of WAFR, I would be called brave and courageous had I done these things—and I am condemned by it since I did not.

These things are set against the call to emulate Christ and his costly love and compassionate justice. Grace and mercy are the patterns of the kingdom of God. God and humanity define *bravery* differently. Both cannot be right.

Therefore, if Jesus is Lord, true bravery is radical obedience and mercy-filled submission to the love of Christ out of an identity truly rooted in him. There is no need to build, project, or protect a false self, because my individual and our collective identities are fixed and unchanging. The call for followers of Jesus and those discipled out of WAFR is the same as it was to Joshua:

> This book of the law shall not depart from your mouth, but you shall meditate on it day and night, so that you may be careful to do according to all that is written in it; for then you will make your way prosperous, and then you will have success. Have I not commanded you? Be strong and courageous! Do not tremble or be dismayed, for the LORD your God is with you wherever you go. (Joshua 1:8-9)

For those who are children of God, the call to courage is to emulate Christ in sacrificial obedience to our good Father. The apostle Paul's conclusion stands in opposition to the dominant narrative peddled by the media and movie producers and perpetuated by our military-industrial complex and militarized police forces. Paul implores followers of Jesus to

> make my joy complete by being of the same mind, maintaining the same love, united in spirit, intent on one purpose. Do nothing from selfishness or empty conceit, but with humility of mind regard one another as more important than yourselves; do not *merely* look out for your own personal interests, but also for the interests of others. . . .
>
> Do all things without grumbling or disputing; so that you will prove yourselves to be blameless and innocent, children of God above reproach in the midst of a crooked and perverse generation, among whom you appear as lights in the world. (Philippians 2:2-4, 14-15)

WAFR contends that bravery is the willingness to be violent—to destroy an enemy at all costs or violate core principles of a self-determined greater good. Contrary to that, bravery for followers of Jesus is an unwavering trust in the profound love of God and the willingness to love sacrificially at all times. Jesus' love drives out all fear, and his abiding presence gives us courage by the power of the Holy Spirit, who dwells among us. When we do not live under the ultimate protection of God, we strive to protect ourselves, risk nothing, and use violence to maintain control.

The followers of WAFR are gripped by the lie that they are the most courageous people on the planet, yet what is actually at work is fear, anxiety, and collective insecurity. WAFR says that Jesus, who commands "Do not let your heart be troubled," (John 14:1) isn't trustworthy because a good guy with a gun or an airstrike isn't on the way. But we who profess Christ say the Lord and his Word alone are trustworthy because Christ is King. Even if we die, we will share in the resurrection. To live and love at all costs is true bravery. People unwavering in their obedience to God, even in the face of violence and suffering, are truly brave.

QUESTIONS FOR INDIVIDUAL REFLECTION AND SMALL GROUP DISCUSSION

- What were your dominant feelings as you read this chapter: curiosity, hope, surprise, confusion, numbness, familiarity, distance, or something else?
- When were those feelings most present?
- What phrases, stories, or historical events resonated with you?
- What events or narratives were you unaware of? What did you learn?
- Where do you disagree or have concerns?
- What questions are you carrying?

REWRITING THE SCRIPTS WE TELL OURSELVES

Many of us grow up with scripts we tell ourselves that are often unhelpful and even destructive. I interpreted from my culture and family that if I expressed fear, sadness, or pain, I was weak.

- What scripts from your home or your culture have you heard about weakness?

- What did your family and friends believe about people who were seen as weak or unable to defend themselves?

- What did it look like in your family or culture to be brave and courageous?

- How does God define bravery (review Joshua's, Esther's, or Paul's description of Jesus)?

- As you begin to redefine bravery, where do you believe God is calling you and what does that look like practically?

  ☐ to be bold and courageous like Joshua

  ☐ to lay down your life like Jesus

  ☐ to be an advocate for the marginalized like Esther

LIE 11

AMERICA IS THE GREATEST COUNTRY ON EARTH

IN 2004, I GRADUATED FROM Park View High School and headed to Columbia University in New York City. I applied to the University of Virginia, Columbia, and New York University without significant guidance or preparation. I wish that I could say from a young age I wanted to attend an elite university, but that's not true. I only knew about UVA because of a summer camp I was privileged to attend via the prompting of my seventh grade science teacher, Mrs. Palmer. And NYU was my safety school because I heard I should have one. I did not know UVA was the number one public university in the United States at the time when I visited there during middle school. And to be honest, I didn't even know what the Ivy League was until twelfth grade. The reason that I applied to Columbia had more to do with my pride than potential.

Early in my senior year, someone said in passing, "I bet you couldn't get into an Ivy League school." I said, "Yes, I can!" totally ignorant of what they were talking about. I resolved to do research when I got home to figure out what the Ivy League was. Thankfully, we had internet access at home, and I typed "Ivy League" and "poetry" into the search bar. Columbia got the first hit. After publishing my first book in 2003, I knew that I wanted to write but had no idea what that looked like professionally. I watched "Def Poetry Jam" on TV, and a lot of those poets were based in New York, so my logic pointed me there.

Hence, my super-specific pre-Google search began and ended quickly. I filled out the essays and applications over a few nights and started on the other requirements.

There were no SAT prep classes, private tutors, or private middle schools or high schools for me. I took the SATs once, and I didn't know anyone else in my high school taking the SAT IIs. I scored 1160 on a 1600 scale, which was well below average compared to my would-be classmates. The average UVA and Columbia scores at the time were 1570. The average for my county, though, was 800. So I guess I was above average for the Southside District. And therein laid my faulty grasp of the world around me.

I was a published author and a varsity high school athlete in three sports. I was holding down one to three jobs to support my family, had a beautiful girlfriend; I didn't have a "baby momma" or criminal record. I thought my life was great, and for an American black male from a broken home, this was a stellar start. Most people around me said as much. My ego was stroked by crowds, and I surrounded myself with people who ensured I felt good about myself. All of this came to a screeching halt at the end of my freshman year at Columbia.

It wasn't a mystery to my professors that I was struggling in my classes. This was especially clear in the core curriculum and particularly literature and humanities. "Lit Hum," as it's known on campus, was the first of two huge courses on majority Western literature. I didn't know how to read five hundred pages a week, write multiple essays at once, or do life far away from anything comfortable and familiar. I was not "special" in this environment, and I stood out for all the wrong reasons.

Before handing in my final paper of freshman year, I distinctly re-member changing the font type and size and adjusting the margins of the document to get to the required page count. On top of that, the core argument of my mock debate between Aristotle and Plato was terrible. Matthew Seidel, my professor and the chair of the department at the time, reviewed this sad attempt before I handed in the in-class portion of our exam. When I walked up to his desk, he looked me in the eyes and said, "You're tired. This summer you need to go back to Brodnax and do whatever you need to do to come back here." Standing there in a cutoff T-shirt from my high school soccer team, gray sweatpants, and sneakers far past their prime, I felt exposed.

This was not Brodnax, Virginia. This was not Park View High School. This was Columbia University in the City of New York. The only thing true about my being the best was that I believed I was. If I was willing to acknowledge the shortcomings of my education, my need for mentorship and development, my lack of critical thinking skills, and the genuine culture shock that exacerbated all of these issues—only then I could truly grow and change. And I don't mean grow and change into someone who was the best or better when compared to others. I mean I needed to develop into someone who was reflective, honest, humble, and willing to learn and serve others even with my limits and needs in full view. This entire predicament through the lens of white American folk religion makes sense. My own sense of validation and value came through work, and that also affected how I valued and prioritized others. I reflected minimally and only slowed down to learn how to work harder and excel in order to reduce my own suffering and discomfort. I rarely admitted or addressed my limitations, opting instead to pretend to be perfect and do whatever it took to protect the false self I projected to the world around me.

MISGUIDED EXCEPTIONALISM

The idea that I am exceptional is not accidental or random, but American to its core. I believed that I had a special purpose that didn't need refinement, only a platform to exert my will. And American exceptionalism claims the same about the United States. America must be the greatest nation on earth and hold a coveted place in God's plan for the universe. This theology is unbiblical and destructive, and the social implications of these beliefs are highly problematic. Conservative author Dinesh D'Souza articulates this stream of thought. John

Winthrop's "city on a hill" claim reasserts itself for the present day in the following excerpts from D'Souza's "10 Great Things" in the *National Review*:

> In most countries in the world, your fate and your identity are handed to you; in America, you determine them for yourself. America is a country where you get to write the script of your own life. Your life is like a blank sheet of paper, and you are the artist. This notion of being the architect of your own destiny is the incredibly powerful idea that is behind the worldwide appeal of America. Young people especially find irresistible the prospect of authoring the narrative of their own lives. . . .
>
> And surely African Americans like Jesse Jackson are vastly better off living in America than they would be if they were to live in, say, Ethiopia or Somalia. America has found a solution to the problem of religious and ethnic conflict that continues to divide and terrorize much of the world. . . .
>
> America, the freest nation on earth, is also the most virtuous nation on earth. . . .
>
> We should love our country not just because it is ours, but also because it is good. America is far from perfect, and there is lots of room for improvement. In spite of its flaws, however, American life as it is lived today is the best life that our world has to offer. Ultimately America is worthy of our love and sacrifice because, more than any other society, it makes possible the good life, and the life that is good.[1]

D'Souza, an Indian immigrant who writes passionately about following Jesus, married his faith to Western ideals, the US Constitution, the Declaration of Independence, and American capitalism. Justice does not roll down in this narrative, but the idea that there is no other place on the planet like the United States trickles down even to its most destitute residents. From D'Souza's perspective, the United States has flaws, but Americans need only be grateful and keep pressing forward because nowhere is better than the Red, White, and Blue. In this narrative, WAFR sets up the United States as the ideal, so the kingdom of God is not. And America's pace of work, lack of reflection, and false grip on reality keep followers moving, with the reminder from evangelists like D'Souza that we are all doing just fine.

We see this assertion especially after police violence or injustice gains significant attention. If there are flaws, the system isn't broken; it was just an isolated incident. Inhabitants of America are still much better off than they would be somewhere else. At its extreme, these ideas are articulated more radically. For example, when referring to slaves in America, D'Souza says in *The End of Racism* that "the American slave was treated like property, which is to say, pretty well."[2] The lie that America is the greatest nation in the world builds on the aforementioned myths and puts itself in opposition to the Jesus of Scripture, his gospel, and the kingdom of God.

The lie that our individual and collective realities are different is exposed in a brief analysis of education in America. In the educational documentary *Waiting for Superman*, the following data was presented:

Since the 1970s US schools have failed to keep pace with the rest of the world. Among thirty developed countries we rank twenty-fifth in math and twenty-first in science. The top 5 percent of [US] students rank twenty-third out of twenty-nine developed countries. In almost every category we have fallen behind except one. The same study looked at math skills that in these eight countries [Korea, Japan, Spain, Germany, France, Australia, Canada] the US ranked last. But when the researchers asked the students how they felt they had done, "Did I get good grades in mathematics?" kids from the USA ranked number one in confidence.[3]

Like my first day sitting in class at Columbia University, I felt ready to contribute and prepared to stand out, but by the end of the year, I accepted that I was not. My graduating class from Park View High

School was the first to have the Standards of Learning implemented. This standardized testing put us on par in the state with much more affluent areas closer to Washington, DC. Many of my classmates, unaware of what this change would mean, reached graduation day and did not receive a diploma but instead a certificate. Many teachers, including my mom, were no longer qualified to do their jobs and struggled to gain newly required certifications. Because salaries for teachers were low, colleges were two to three hours away, and many of the teachers were products of the previously segregated and still under-resourced schools they now taught in, these new certifications were simply out of reach.

Ultimately, my mom lost her job and had to find another teaching position in North Carolina. Mecklenburg County still struggles to adequately prepare its students and teachers for academic excellence, yet the perception of their preparedness is still far from the reality they exist in. My county is not an exception but the rule in America, and the dominant narrative that "we are the best," is challenged by citizens for whom things are not turning out as they hoped.

A HIGHER IDEAL

Without acknowledgment, there can be no confession. And without confession, there can be no repentance. Without repentance, there is no change of direction. And so, without this reorientation, justice isn't possible. Thus the personal, relational, and systemic reconciliation and renewal that all of creation longs for is perpetually out of reach. In contrast, acknowledgment of our limits, confession of our brokenness, and turning toward redemption through an encounter with Jesus to pursue righteousness and justice is central to Christianity. The result of this personal and corporate confession is the present and eternal wholeness and shalom that God originally intended.

Therefore, it is not just that America believes it is exceptional that is problematic, but the idea coupled with the strident resistance to reflection, repentance, and submission to God makes it sinful.

Either Jesus reigns or we do. WAFR and the presence of God are not just two different theories but completely different kingdoms to be realized. Every person that has ever lived will have the opportunity to choose life with an idol or life with God.

WAFR's idol is America, and it declares to all that the United States is the "greatest country on the planet" and all humanity's ultimate dwelling place. Jesus declares that life with him and the people of God in the beautiful city of God is what we were ultimately made for.

We see this clearly when putting George Washington's first inaugural address next to Jesus' first sermon in John 4. In 1789, Washington stood before the Senate and House of Representatives and delivered a speech laying out his vision for both the presidency and the nation. After brief opening remarks, Washington offered praise and appreciation to God and claimed divine connections between the destiny of the United States, the world, and his historical moment:

> In obedience to the public summons, repaired to the present station, it would be peculiarly improper to omit in this first official act my fervent supplications to that Almighty Being who rules over the universe, who presides in the councils of nations, and whose providential aids can supply every human defect, that his benediction may consecrate to the liberties and happiness of the people of the United States a Government instituted by themselves for these essential purposes, and may enable every instrument employed in its administration to execute with success the functions allotted to his charge.[4]

It is apparent that Washington firmly believed that God's providential hands were on the men in the room. And he claimed that he can hardly contain his thankfulness to God, saying these reflections were too "strongly on my mind to be suppressed." Therefore, the racial, gender, and class-based hierarchy, along with land theft and genocide of Native Americans and enslavement of Africans that made this momentous occasion possible were no doubt God's "providential agency" guided by his "invisible hand." Additionally, there is no doubt that Washington's personal experience was the opposite of the "tranquil deliberations and voluntary consent of so many distinct communities" he claims to be responsible for the formation of this new nation. His two to three hundred slaves, the Iroquois that were skinned from the hips down after defeat under his watch, and the seventy-five thousand men wounded and maimed in the Revolutionary War would likely disagree with his assessment.[5] Still, though, he claimed there is no better circumstance for a nation of such promise and blessing to begin. Washington continued to assert the supposed divine nature of the United States' past, present, and future:

> The propitious smiles of heaven can never be expected on a nation that disregards the eternal rules of order and right which heaven itself has ordained; and since the preservation of the sacred fire of liberty and the destiny of the republican model of government are justly considered, perhaps, as deeply, as finally, staked on the experiment entrusted to the hands of the American people.

Consistent with the Declaration of Independence and the Constitution, Washington endorses the republic, the role of the US government, and strident patriotism. But he goes a step further and calls it ordained by heaven. Since Washington and his white, wealthy, male comrades were able to have the things they worked so hard for, there is no doubt that God ordained it to be this way. Thus, "preservation of the sacred fire of liberty and the destiny of the republican model" as entrusted to them (white, male, wealthy) is the highest calling and must never be abandoned. This marriage of power and favor on the precondition of sexuality, gender, race, wealth, and effort, along with nationalism, is the foundation and core of WAFR and is embodied in the first president of the United States. Per Washington and those who adopt this unbiblical belief and perspective, this is what makes the United States the greatest nation on earth.

The kingdom of God and the gospel of Jesus Christ is altogether different.

THE LORD'S FAVOR

In Luke 4:14-20, Jesus gives an account of who he is, what he's come to do, and who sent him. After Jesus was baptized by John the Baptist and tempted by Satan, he returned to Galilee in the power of the Spirit. He taught in the temple, and word got out that something unique was happening—someone special was there. He entered the temple in his hometown, and while everyone was looking at him, he said:

> The Spirit of the Lord is upon Me,
> Because He anointed Me to preach the gospel to the poor.
> He has sent Me to proclaim release to the captives,
> And recovery of sight to the blind,
> To set free those who are oppressed,
> To proclaim the favorable year of the Lord. (Luke 4:18-19)

This is similar to George Washington's address in some key ways.

Like Washington, Jesus connected himself and his actions to the divine plan of God. Jesus also hearkened back to the prophet Isaiah, using a passage that those gathered in the temple would have known, just like when Washington paraphrased some of the Declaration of Independence and culturally well-known religious phrases. Both of them declared what they were aiming to do and what it would accomplish. It's likely that even their audiences were a bit similar. Likely surrounding Jesus were men of power, wealth, and those who benefited from the structures of society, just like Washington was surrounded by wealthy, well-connected, white men. This is where the similarities end.

Jesus did not pander to or prioritize the people in his midst as Washington did. Jesus did not affirm the way things were occurring among the Jewish people at the time or rebuke the Roman occupation. He did not double down on his commitment to the status quo; nor did he proclaim that the men gathered there were favored by God and thus would continue the lifestyle they enjoyed. His address prioritized certain people—the poor, the oppressed, prisoners, and the disabled. Some of these people were not even allowed into the temple! Jesus also proclaimed the year of the Lord's favor, which is a reference back to Leviticus 25, where God proclaims four key realities:

- *freedom* for all who were held captive as slaves or prisoners
- *restoration* of all that had been lost, stolen, or forfeited
- *favor*—receiving the provision and protection of the Lord
- *rest*—both naturally (e.g., fields, animals) and spiritually[6]

Under the rule and reign of Christ, slaves and prisoners will be set free, and whatever was obtained unjustly is to be restored. People will be healed from disease and receive blessings of provision and protection. And for all, including the land and animals, there will be rest from all work and labor. Later in Luke 4, Jesus began to do what he said he would do by casting out demons, healing the sick, and preaching the kingdom of God.

Contrary to Jesus, Washington promoted and perpetuated slavery and systems of oppression that grew, changed, and persist to this day. The economic system he championed has only expanded its exploitation of the planet's people and resources. He told his comrades that the path they were on was righteous, just, and good, while he twisted Scripture to prove these points. The implications of Washington's speech and actions are entirely antithetical to the message of Christ. American exceptionalism is a tempting but unsatisfying idea.

All of us have to choose who we will serve. We can worship at the altar of work and performance for a reward. Or we can rest in Christ and work in response to the reception of our reward in full as we are adopted into the family of God and filled with the Holy Spirit by his glorious grace. The myth of American exceptionalism and the lie that *America is the greatest country in the world* is the extension of the individual belief that *I am the best*. And no person can bear this burden of superiority and supremacy, except for Christ.

Humility, not pride, marks faithful followers of Jesus, and choosing humility leads to life's most beautiful and transformative moments. This occurs every time men confess ignorance and complicity in society's war against women. Or when US citizens move from condemnation to advocacy for undocumented people. Or, in the ultimate rebuke of idolatry, when someone confesses their sin and asks Jesus to be the savior they cannot be for themselves.

FROM EXCEPTIONALISM TO CONFESSION

While reading Salma Hayek's "Harvey Is My Monster Too" in the *New York Times*, I found myself forced to choose between the pridefulness of WAFR—which tempts me to think, *I am so much better than those men over there*—or humility and repentance, confessing my complicity in her exploitation.[7] Reading her tragic account, I could only think of my contribution to her abuse. I could not muster anger at Harvey Weinstein, only disappointment in myself that my young eyes too had made her less than human.

After Mrs. Hayek recounted Weinstein's retaliation because of her rejection of his sexual advances, she said this of her abuser: "In his eyes, I was not an artist. I wasn't even a person. I was a thing: not a nobody, but a body." This is true of Weinstein, but it was also true of me.

Frida was a stunningly beautiful film starring Hayek, and I watched it when it premiered in 2002. But I didn't watch it because I wanted to learn more about Frida Kahlo. I watched it because it was rated R for sexuality and nudity. I could not tell you what *Desperado* (1995) was about, but I could tell you that Hayek was in it. And intellectually I could make a case for why a guy like me would be interested in both of those films but if I am honest, the plot was irrelevant. I am guilty of reducing Hayek to a body, and I confess and repent. Because to do that to a woman made in the image of God is a violation of her humanity and God's grand purposes for both of us.

There is a vast, silent group of men and women who financially sustained what Weinstein did for decades. And a large and growing number of men and women are willing to pay for more as the use of pornography continues to grow, while music videos and other media follow the same dollars. Further eroticization continues as the entertainment industry makes billions of dollars by reducing human beings to bodies that men and women like me consume. Flesh is auctioned and sold as art and entertainment, and many are willing to pay, as I did. I clicked on ads that made money for a company that made sure more cleavage was seen in the sidebar of my screen. Totally unnecessary scenes in movie trailers geared toward men like me get us to buy tickets to the theater, hit play on the internet videos, or stay up late watching Cinemax.

I am not exceptional. There are too many holes in my case for greatness. And neither can America claim to be the greatest country, because only God and his purposes are great. Sexual exploitation is essential to this nation, but it is not part of his kingdom. There are two options: confess and repent, or justify ourselves and mount a defense of our own righteousness. Paul chose to confess and repent, allowing Christ to be his righteousness (Philippians 3:3-14). The key word for me throughout Philippians 3 is the word *flesh*.

Flesh is not referring to Paul's physical body per se but indicates an internal disposition linked to where Paul put his trust. He resisted the urge to stand on his ethnic heritage, cultural identity, citizenship, education, class, or accomplishments for justification. Paul knew that these things could not bear the weight of his identity. Instead he chose full reliance on Christ. He chose not to walk in the false self but in the fullness of the Spirit. Paul's greatness is bound up in the greatness of Christ. Thus he can embrace the faults he has because his status doesn't change, and followers of Jesus can do the same thing. Even more, we can point out the faults around us without judgment or condemnation but with compassion and justice by acknowledging our individual and collective weakness and calling all to true strength in Christ.

In WAFR, it is not possible to acknowledge weakness, practice confession, and repent to receive the forgiveness, acceptance, and mercy from God. In WAFR, a person must work for it. But in the kingdom of God individual and corporate confession and repentance are essential disciplines and mark the lives of true children of God.

QUESTIONS FOR INDIVIDUAL REFLECTION AND SMALL GROUP DISCUSSION

- What were your dominant feelings as you read this chapter: curiosity, hope, surprise, confusion, numbness, familiarity, distance, or something else?

- When were those feelings the most present?

- What phrases, stories, or historical events resonated with you?

- What events or narratives were you unaware of? What did you learn?

- Where do you disagree or have concerns?

- What questions are you carrying?

WE MUST BE CLEANSED BY GOD TO BE SENT BY GOD

There is nothing we can do for God to love us any more or any less. Read Isaiah 6:1-8. If you were to have an encounter with Jesus, knowing that he knows everything about you already and loves you anyway, what would you bring to him that you might be clean? Write it down as if you were writing a letter to God.

Then, turn to Psalm 103 and reflect on the forgiveness of God and his mercy toward us. What verses stand out to you and why?

Go back to Isaiah 6 and read the whole chapter.

After Isaiah confessed, he was blessed and sent. Isaiah confessed that he was a man of unclean lips, and as the prophet to the people, this is the core of his daily life. Yet God doesn't take his position away but instead sends him back to speak. Go back and read what you confessed.

- How might God want to use your cleansing to proclaim the greatness of his name?
- Who might God be sending you to?
- What would be your message to them?

LIE 12

WE ARE ONE NATION

THE FIRST TIME I PERFORMED "We, Too," I thought that I was going to explode. When the lights came up on the stage, it was like a pin was pulled from a grenade and I blew up. I have never felt I fit into the fabric of this country, though my ancestors picked the cotton that put it together. But I had neither articulated it before nor been validated by applause from an audience of hundreds of people from all parts of the world at the same time.

We, Too

My skin speaks volumes my mouth may never say
sends messages my mind may never know
writes pages a pen in my palm never wrote
my skin . . .
brown but called black—
a whip cracks my mental back
my head aches from self-hate
that I want to go away
My skin says,
I may have struggled but my grandmother definitely did.
some white man, somewhere
had an illegitimate, illegal kid
My cousins passed with green eyes and light skin
but my granddaddy dark,
walked up to doors and couldn't get in . . .

he wanted to buy land in Southern Virginia
but couldn't because of my skin
For some it's a source of pride
for me, I find it hard to stay unashamed
as I'm asked are you Ghanaian, Dominican, or Haitian?
and my response disrespects my ancestors when I say,
I'm just black.
Uttered from under a cloud of adversity, whispered from
behind the shadow of struggle
I'm just black . . .
I want to say it with more something
but all I hear are Asian parents telling Asian daughters not to
date me
older generations fighting inclinations not to hate me
They say once you go black you never go back
but that's only half the fact,
once you go black you never go back because some white men
won't let you
I think black and I think pain
and I want so bad for my thoughts to change
but a world when I'm equal is just a dream
dreamt by a minority ruled by an indifferent majority
leaving me somewhere between radical Afrocentrism
or racial indifference with no ethnic identity at all . . .
Society won't let me remember the Nat Turners or the Nat
King Coles
because I just might find my pride, grab my ax, hack out a path
to justice
all while singing we shall overcome. . . .
I must recall the slave in me
so I can fight for those minds that aren't yet free
free to hope, free to dream
Yes we can, is the song that I sing

and I'll keep singing until the world is singing with me
They don't want me to remember the Martins or the Malcolms
because minds like mine start movements
Bunche, Banneker, Carver, Powell, Douglass,
Marshall, Ali, Angelou, Kersey, Washington, Wheatley,
Lewis, Walker, they are within me and I must remember . . .
Biko, Mandela, Aquino, Tubman, Truth—
I must remember the truth
that we must be measured by much more than our
levels of melanin
and our children won't know our history unless we continue to
tell them
that the greatest race is the human race and we must flock
with runners like
Lincoln, Lennon, Locke, Gandhi, Tutu, Mead, living in one
world, in one great country.
because we too, sing America.
We are dark, light, black, yellow, brown and white
all fighting for the amnesty of the mind
They send us to eat in the kitchen
When company comes,
But we laugh,
And eat well,
And grow strong.
Tomorrow,
we'll be at the table
When company comes.
Nobody'll dare
Say to us,
"Eat in the kitchen,"
Then.
Besides,
They'll see how beautiful we are

And be ashamed—
we, too, are America.

This poem, inspired by Langston Hughes's "I, Too," highlights a particularly painful tension that my skin and blood embody. I inhabit a
country my people were brought to, and now that we are no longer
slaves we struggle to find a place to truly fit, or, maybe better, those
who brought us here can't agree on a place to put us. Yet amid all that
my people have and continue to endure, I'm supposed to stand for its
anthem and pledge allegiance.

I am sure that I am one man, but I don't believe that the United
States is one nation—nor do I believe that should be my highest hope
or our greatest goal. This places me in firm opposition to white
American folk religion and cements my place in the family of Jesus.

THE CALL FOR CONFORMITY

To affirm that America is one nation is to propose that I, an African
American male, am valuable and belong in this country. And the same
would have to be said of every person holding citizenship; they too
must receive the same fair, just, and equal opportunity and treatment.
But the past and present inequities make that point impossible to
prove. There has never been a moment of my life when I felt that type
of wholehearted, national inclusion. Instead, there was an insistence
on editing my people's history or excluding from it altogether.

I remember the look of the white father who threatened me in the
ball pit when I was six years old at McDonald's in South Hill, Virginia,
after playfully hitting his daughter with a plastic ball. That's the same
look I received after my fifth-grade Christmas program at LaCrosse
Elementary School when I hugged another white man's daughter
goodbye. The look of disapproval, disgust, and silent warning is with
me to this day. When I was in eighth grade, a white female classmate
said, "I think everyone should just stay with their own kind." And in
eleventh grade, I found out my friend's stepfather violently beat his
mother when he found out she had dated a black man. Familial

disapproval, social rejection, and even violence were consequences for getting too close to people who looked like me.

I cannot remember a time when I didn't think that if a woman chose to date or marry me, it wouldn't mean giving up her family. And that was true for Priscilla when she chose to marry me. She had to be willing to commit a social, cultural, and economic sin, and join herself to a man with brown skin darkened by generations of sexual abuse and labor exploitation—the hallmarks of slavery. She had to be willing as a Chinese-Korean American woman to follow the Jesus of Scripture and his invitation to life in his kingdom, and resist the idol of WAFR that beckons her toward the *best* opportunities for life, liberty, and happiness. And the enduring beliefs and testimony of WAFR are that blackness certainly can't and won't lead to anything positive, sustainable, or better. Being seen as black is a step down, a step back, and a step off the ladder of America's promise and the vision of most immigrant Chinese and Korean families. This race-based scale is well documented, well-defined, and well-established as the acceptable and promoted norm. Yet every true follower of Jesus must renounce this system and recognize every person as being made in the image of God and worthy of inclusion in the family of Jesus and a seat at our tables for dinner every night.

But in spite of all that, WAFR calls us to affirm that we are "one nation" and pledge allegiance to that false truth. In spite of racially biased sentencing, racial resegregation of school districts, and increased voter suppression, this false faith claims we are a large family with common goals, values, and destiny.[1] And when that twisted reality is called into question, the powers of this world say we must at least honor those that protect the opportunity to be supposedly free. We see this in the hearty debate around protests in the United States today. And reading through dialogues and arguments by academics, athletes, politicians, activists, and Facebook users, it is safe to deduce that there is no acceptable way to protest and dispute the oneness that's professed but doesn't exist.

That's because WAFR demands devotion to its goals and conformity to its perspective. And both of these demands—devotion and conformity—are dismissive, dishonest, destructive, and woefully inadequate to address humanity's deepest needs.

When we resist the dominant collective reality and publicly disagree, we will be harassed online, as I and many others can attest. It also means the possibility of being assaulted verbally and physically, and losing our jobs and livelihoods. I remember the first time I was threatened. I was in North Carolina speaking against labor and sexual slavery in a room with one hundred people. Someone wrote on one of the response envelopes that I should never come back, and if I knew what was good for me I would stop altogether. Threats and intimidation are not new, special, or one-offs. This is evidenced on a wider scale by the assault of a protester at the urging of President Trump in 2016, and Trump's words to NFL players who refused to stand during the national anthem to protest police brutality.[2]

James Franklin McGraw sucker punched Rakeem Jones in the face at a Trump campaign rally in Fayetteville, North Carolina, on March 9, 2016. Jones was protesting at the rally and being escorted out by police when McGraw stepped out of his seat and punched Jones in the face. The police then threw Jones to the ground, placed him in handcuffs, and removed him from the arena. McGraw went back to his seat unbothered, unrepentant, and received a pat of approval from the woman next to him. Immediately after the rally McGraw responded to a series of questions about whether or not he liked the rally and if the protester deserved the punch. McGraw said, "You bet I liked it. . . . Knocking the hell out of that big mouth. We don't know who he is, but we know he's not acting like an American. . . . He deserved it. The next time we see him, we might have to kill him."[3]

There were polar opposite responses to this incident. They included condemnation by some and celebration by others. This highlights the stark contrast between those who feel at home in America, those who feel they are losing the home they love, and those trying to make a home in the United States. These sentiments have always been present. America may claim and aspire to unity and oneness, but the lived experiences of those who reside here show the opposite is true. The Trump campaign and presidency brought these divisions out of the shadows and into the light and he used them for his political advantage, but these divisions have been here all along.

Throughout the political primary and 2016 campaign season, and consistently in the wake of Trump's presidency as of this writing, the threat of retribution for withholding faithful support for, or offering critique of, WAFR America has been standard operating procedure. This tactic was used again on September 23, 2017, when Trump tweeted, "Wouldn't you love to see one of these NFL owners, when somebody disrespects our flag, to say, 'Get that son of a bitch off the field right now? Out! He's fired. He's fired!'"[4]

Nearly three people per day were killed by police in 2017.[5] A disproportionate number of these killings occurred within the African American community. And African American men make up the majority of the National Football League. The willingness of the Trump administration and wealthy owners to inflict more damage is profoundly troubling. What Trump is doing, though, is not new, unique, or exclusively Republican. Those who claim to be on the political left of American politics engage in the same type of behavior with the same rigor, intensity, and real-life consequences.

Matthew Hutson offers valuable insight in his article "Why Liberals Aren't as Tolerant as They Think."[6] At Middlebury College, white supremacist Charles Murray was shouted down by students and activists in March 2016. He is most famous for his 1994 book *The Bell Curve*, which links socioeconomic status to race and gender.

Prior to that, journalist Wes Enzinna chronicled the infamous clash between antiracist groups and a gathering of white supremacists in 2012.

At lunchtime on May 19, 2012, 18 masked men and women shouldered through the front door of the Ashford House restaurant in Tinley Park, Illinois, a working-class suburb of

Chicago. Some diners mistook the mob for armed robbers. Others thought they might be playing a practical joke. But Steven Speers, a stalactite-bearded 33-year-old who had just sat down for appetizers at a white nationalist meet and greet, had a hunch who they were. The gang filing in with baseball bats, police batons, hammers, and nunchucks were members of Anti-Racist Action (ARA) and the Hoosier Anti-Racist Movement (HARM), two groups dedicated to violently confronting white supremacists.[7]

Enzinna drills down into the backgrounds of those leading this anti-racist movement, drawing clear pictures of the diverse ethnic communities these white men were exposed to but also the poverty of opportunity and lack of identity that surrounded most of them. Additionally, in the article "Left Hook" Enzinna traces the violent back and forths between radical left and radical right groups, which include the shootings and stabbings of neo-Nazis and Klansmen decades ago as well as protesters of waging war against white supremacy stretching from pre-World War I to today.[8] We cannot be one with those we are attempting to harm or destroy.

FAITH AND ALLEGIANCE

WAFR is different from Christianity as practiced in the early church. WAFR does not require followers to reflect, confess, repent, or seek justice as determined by God. Instead, WAFR demands an unwavering commitment to maintaining humanity's status quo of working for identity and inclusion based on a scale that includes race, gender, class, status, and education. The Pledge of Allegiance reads: "I pledge allegiance to the flag of the United States of America, and to the Republic for which it stands, one Nation under God, indivisible, with liberty and justice for all."[9]

WAFR necessitates faith, hope, and trust in the United States though deep unacknowledged and unresolved divisions persist and justice for all has never happened. Whether it is the lines between the rich and the poor, men and women, ethnic groups, or political and religious factions in this country, the appeal stands that "we are all Americans" (one nation). And since that's the case, we must ascribe to a particular set of ideals and beliefs that if wholeheartedly adopted will bring about the change we believe in and the utopia that we were made for.

In modern history there is not a leader more capable of articulating the gospel of America as the hope for the world than Barack Obama. His speech on February 5, 2008, was an epic invitation to a divided people to reconcile without seeking or receiving Christlike justice, to put bitterness aside without grieving pain, and to heal without corporate acknowledgement of the hurt of so many.[10] In the midst of a contentious race with then Senator Hillary Clinton, he began these remarks by naming specific cross-sections of society traditionally at odds with one another and calling those assembled to a collective vision of a more open future with life, liberty, and the pursuit of happiness available to everyone.

Obama's speech painted a picture of America that minimized the deep fractures of society while drawing a clear line to the possibility of a better world. Of course, he did not denounce or reject the present system, but instead suggested the system's true values were not being lived out to their full potential. Therefore, *we* should double down, join him, and work harder in the democratic, generous, melting pot where we all experience the freedom fought for by so many brave men and women before us. Obama asserted that this moment, this people, and this country are unique, and American's certainly are up to the task of making a better world for ourselves and our children.

In reality, the United States is a far cry from being united, and Obama and others would certainly acknowledge that fact in 2016. But this disunity has always been true. The United States is "one nation" only in opinion and perspective, not reality. It's more accurate that we are the divided states of America in a united state of amnesia, choosing not to remember what's happened to pursue the unity we crave.

We work for something, and there is the illusion of progress. And a valiant effort to end conflict and suffering as quickly as possible feels better than to merely accept it. This is especially true in a society that worships work and longs for a hero. The United States seems to believe that if we as a people just try harder to be happy, create our own best life now, and fight to protect the freedoms we supposedly have, oneness will materialize. That hasn't proved to be true and never will be.

ONE KINGDOM

Everyone under the reign of WAFR is judged by their level of productivity. Since work is how people are measured, overwork becomes the norm. Thus, we are too busy seeking to excel to reflect on the fruits of our labors or the lack of it. WAFR rolls out a red carpet for what appears to be all comers, regardless of background. That welcome mat quickly turns into a treadmill where some are embraced immediately and others are not, but every person must work to keep up, keep their place, or be left behind. Contrast that with living in the family of God. The way of Jesus is Sabbath rest, daily rhythms, and delight in him, because then we see him and ourselves rightly. The disunity comes to the surface, the limits of this world are clear, and our need for something more is revealed before us. The idol of WAFR won't fill it, but the kingdom of God does. Slowing down to see the life and death of my mom, I saw this fully.

Leo Tolstoy's *Anna Karenina* opens with the line, "All happy families are alike; each unhappy family is unhappy in its own way."[11] And that is true of my family as well. When my mom died of cancer and I took the podium after my two brothers to finish her eulogy, I decided to do a call to faith in Jesus. My mother worked her whole life knowing that she lived in a country that didn't want her. She longed for a kingdom that had not yet come in full. And those gathered in the room would never see her again unless they knew her Savior.

Yes, she was part of the VFW Women's Auxiliary, but they were not of one mind. Yes, she was part of Mecklenburg and Halifax County Public Schools, but they were not of one heart. Yes, she was part of the Walton-Allen family, but we were not all of one hope. Yes, all of the people in that room loved her in some way as best as they could, but their love and best wishes for her did not mean they were of one faith. The oneness that my mother longed for is the oneness that Jesus prayed and laid down his life for as recorded in John 17:1-24.

I believe Ma received in part in her life, and in full in her death the oneness Jesus prayed for. And her experience of joining with God will be experienced by every follower of Jesus, myself included. This full adoption into the family of God shatters any other system of identification, value, and dignity. This obliteration of division includes racial hierarchy, nation-state, and status based on our individual work, effort, or affiliation. Over and above all the walls and lines that were used to exclude my mom from an education, economic security, and certain neighborhoods sits a Savior at the right hand of God who laid down his life and rose from the grave. And by his power she will be raised to live with Him. In Christ, all dividing walls of hostility were brought down and overcome. What WAFR promises but can never deliver is realized in full for those who opt out of the pursuit of their own life, liberty, and happiness, and dive headfirst into the grace of God.

Obama was not able to lead us to the reality he spoke of because he was not the Messiah. *He* was not who we were waiting for and neither are *we*. The truth is that the country he cast vision for doesn't exist because no country, including America, is a replacement for the kingdom of God. And thus the present (or coming) reconciliation and oneness claimed for America is a false gospel, an untruth, and not good news to anyone. This type of endless work for identity and place leads to weariness, unfulfillment, cynicism, and spiritual death.

America's false unity is an expensive pursuit that the false perception of American togetherness can never afford. Unprocessed oppression cost the colonizer just as much if not more than those colonized because both groups lose their humanity, purpose, and identity. White supremacy deifies white people and demonizes all others. Both are acts of dehumanization.

Our current culture lives in the shadow of these divisions, and those in power are unwilling to bring them into the light. Thus the lie endures, so the oppressed and the oppressors who refuse to face the pain and conflict for freedom in Jesus remain in darkness.

On a relational level the lie that "we are one nation" is particularly harmful because it dismisses the history of the many Native nations present in the United States. Additionally, it paints imperialists, human traffickers, explorers, refugees, slaves, and true immigrants with one broad, subjective brush. Systemically, it is painfully inaccurate to say we are *one nation* in the wake of continued educational inequality, segregation by race and class, mass incarceration, and other ills sustained by our inability to reconcile our historical divisions.

Jesus said we will be known by the fruit we bear (Matthew 7:15-20). It is impossible for bad seeds to bear good fruit, and the seeds of this country are exploitative, dehumanizing, and oppressive. Therefore, neither this country's founders nor its citizens today hold the character and capacity necessary to atone for our collective brokenness or to reconcile us to ourselves, our history, and creation. WAFR would have us believe that we can deliver this reality for ourselves by ourselves. But Paul says the opposite:

> For it is by grace [God's remarkable compassion and favor drawing you to Christ] that you have been saved [actually delivered from judgment and given eternal life] through faith. And this [salvation] is not of yourselves [not through your own effort], but it is the [undeserved, gracious] gift of God; not as a result of [your] works [nor your attempts to keep the Law], so that no one will [be able to] boast *or* take credit in any way [for his salvation]. (Ephesians 2:8-9 AMP)

Furthermore, when we minimize our differences in relationships, we are unable to celebrate the distinctive gifts God gave to all ethnicities, cultures, and backgrounds. In Genesis, Acts, and Revelation, we see the beloved community God created, began again, and ultimately brings to himself. We are many nations in the United States, and that, according to Scripture, is not just a good thing but how it was meant to be.

Humanity's common denominator is that we are all made in the image of God (Genesis 1:27). This, of course, includes Gentiles. In Acts 10 God speaks clearly to Peter through a vision. In it God compels Peter, the rock on which God will build his church, not to call any person unclean that God has made clean. Therefore, all who choose to deny themselves, take up their cross, and follow him (Matthew 16:24-25) are adopted into the family of God. Finally, in Revelation 7 we see every tribe, tongue, and nation joined together not by political ideology, skin color, or economic status but by relationship with the Son of God.

According to Scripture, the oneness with God and others that we long for is innate in every person. God confers to us an identity all can fully embrace when we become his children through Christ. The kingdom of God is an eternal, unchanging reality of unity under the rule and reign of a just, loving Father. WAFR calls us to be an idolatrous nation with liberty and justice defined by ourselves and imposed on others. But Christ invites us into God's family with liberty and justice defined by him and an opportunity to invite others. Under the idol of America, our identity must be earned. Under God, our identity is given.

WAFR distances itself from those who (1) don't fit the mold of perfection, (2) resist the status quo, (3) embody difference, and (4) don't seek to meet the social standards of dominant culture. We see this is in families, churches, and institutions that shut their doors to teenage mothers, ostracize those with mental illness, fear those who are LGBTQIA+, and shun those who struggle with addiction.

And those are the people Jesus is closest to. He comes close to all those who are broken, imperfect, and alone. He chooses solidarity with the rejected. He does not promise hope and change, but is hope and change itself. We cannot be the hope we've been waiting for and trust in the hope of Christ at the same time. Either he is the hope of the world or we are. Therefore, to claim to be one with the idol of America and to be one with Christ is a lie. To choose Christ is to choose truth and life.

My mother chose life with God as she was leaving this world. I know this because after not speaking for nearly forty-eight hours and being immersed in the singing of Negro spirituals and hymns, she finished the chorus of a song adapted from Psalm 127. The national anthem, the Pledge of Allegiance, or the Preamble to the Declaration of Independence weren't etched on her heart or the first things that came to mind as cancer ravaged her body. Her last words were the words of God and praises to him:

> The Lord is my light and my salvation
> The Lord is my light and my salvation
> The Lord is my light and my salvation
> Whom shall I fear?
> You just wait on the Lord and be of good courage
> You just wait on the Lord and be of good courage
> You just wait on the Lord and be of good courage
> He will strengthen your heart
> In the times of trouble, He will hide me
> In the times of trouble, He will hide me
> In the times of trouble, He will hide me
> The Lord is my light and my salvation
> The Lord is my light and my salvation
> The Lord is my light and my salvation
> Whom shall I fear?[12]

This is a picture of a life oriented around the love of Jesus and abiding in Christ, not WAFR. A heart, mind, and spirit cannot bow down to both.

CONCLUSION

LEAVING OUR NETS TO FOLLOW JESUS

THE TWELVE LIES DISCUSSED in this book are the core beliefs that keep the idol of white American folk religion in place. These lies dominate dinner conversations and induce anxiety and stress during the holidays. These twelve underlying assumptions keep critique at bay, shush dissonance, and lead to the destruction of our planet and the death of people who are downstream of our misuse of wealth and power.

Fortunately, there is a space for prayerful, sustainable resistance and emotionally healthy activism that includes community and freedom through full adoption into the family of Jesus. It must be said that if we decide to follow the Jesus of Scripture and live differently, we will stand out and be opposed. After all, Jesus promises persecution for his disciples (Mark 10:30), and Paul warns, "Woe to you when everyone speaks well of you" (Luke 6:26 NIV). Family members, friends, our community, and American Christian culture will ask questions, and some will push back to varying degrees. Few will question our desire to build a bigger home, move to a safer neighborhood, or pursue higher pay for the sake of comfort, stability, and security because it is consistent with the WAFR and the culture they know. But we are called by God to bear witness to his kingdom, not our culture or country.

In Luke 9 Jesus calls us to take up our cross daily, deny ourselves, and follow him. Therefore, it is not radical or drastic to confront these twelve lies, remain prayerfully resistant, and obey our good shepherd in word, deed, and power. This is what it means to be a disciple and follower of Jesus.

Jesus paid the ultimate price for resisting the cultures of the day, as did many of his apostles and many martyrs yet today. Jesus invites us, just as he did the first disciples, to put down our nets and pursue a life with him (Luke 5). This invitation and the Great Commission have not changed.

Leaving your nets to follow Jesus requires childlike faith. You might wonder, *What do I do now?* I've asked that question as well. And if everyone who flipped through these pages took the same three action steps, we would be missing the point. Following Jesus is about engaging the messiness of this world with the beauty of the risen King, not creating structures to avoid feelings of discomfort, powerlessness, and uncertainty.

Every Christian has access to the living God, and can hear from him and respond to him. Every person is made in the image of God to flourish, work, rule, and create. And through Christ we can receive healing and freedom, and then reflect that shalom in community and bear witness to him. So my sincere desire is that like Peter, after you have already fished, you would push your boat out to deep water to fish again at a time of day that makes no sense. That you would be faithful and obedient because Jesus isn't just Savior but Lord. And then, sitting in the presence of God, filled with the Spirit, wait and see the cross he has for you to bear.

My longing is for you, individually and in community, to have an encounter with Christ that leads you, like Isaiah, to confession, repentance, cleansing, and sending—over and over again. My deep hope is that you would fast like Esther and mourn like Mordecai when you hear of the vulnerable being violated, and go to the king like Nehemiah because your city must be restored.

Remember that Peter did not put down his nets because he received a detailed proposal of what the kingdom of God was offering in comparison to the business plan of the Pharisees and Romans. He left his job because he found abundant life. Peter decided to stop trusting what he could see and put faith in a kingdom that had not yet come because Jesus showed up. Deep down, he longed for the liberation of the Jewish people from the oppression of Rome. Peter and the Jewish people of the day were looking for a Messiah to lead them in political liberation. Ultimately, though, he was given a freedom that neither the religious authorities nor the Caesars could take away.

When he left his boat, Peter did not know his mother-in-law would be healed of a fever by Christ. He did not know that Lazarus would be raised from the dead. And he certainly didn't know that he too would cast out demons and heal the sick. Yet he still put down his nets to learn from and live with Jesus.

I don't know what God has in store for you when you turn away from pursuing comfort, stability, and security to ground your identity in the family of Jesus. But I do know he will be with you and you will lack nothing.

I don't know what will happen when you confront the racism, sexism, and classism in your family, peer group, and community (after you confess it in your own heart). But I do know that he will never leave or forsake you. I don't know what will happen when you show up to work and realize God is calling you to reflect shalom on the base, at the precinct, in the classroom, behind the steering wheel, or in your cubicle. I don't know what you should do when you step into the ballot box or open the door to your pastor's office to talk about your holy discontent with how the church is responding to sexual assault and gender violence in your faith community. But I do know that Jesus will be with you, and your success is not measured by the healing of every person you pray for, the baptism of every person you preach to, or the passing of every law you push for. It will be in your faithful obedience as his witness in every corner of creation.

So, will you put down your nets? Not because you know what's going to happen but because Jesus is Lord, our God is good, and the Holy Spirit is within you.

ACKNOWLEDGMENTS

THANK YOU TO EVERYONE up and down Allen Road in Brodnax, Virginia, who loved me and formed me when I was young. And thanks to the many women and men from Virginia to New York who claimed me as their son. I appreciate you!

My deep thanks also to all of my friends and colleagues in InterVarsity Christian Fellowship, especially Ashley Byrd for calling me to Jesus, Brunel Bienvenu for always requesting me as his roommate, and Emily Craig for doing a lot more than being an administrative assistant. The presence of IVCF NY/NJ in my life reminds me of the power of a praying mother.

A specials thanks to my wife, Priscilla, along with Pete and Geri Scazzero, Dr. Charles Bershatsky, Alan and Elissa Lin-Rathe, Carolyn Carney and David Larabee, Orlando and Maritza Crespo, Marten and Valeria Hoekstra, and Jason and Sophia Gaboury for creating sacred space for me to feel seen, heard, and safe. Without you, none of this would be possible.

And to Al Hsu and InterVarsity Press, thank you for the opportunity to write this book and your partnership in pressing into the presence of God for knowledge, wisdom, and a deeper sense of his leading. Thank you!

Last and most important, all praise and thanks to God our Father, because apart from him I am nothing, but with Christ, I am made whole.

APPENDIX 1

"WHERE I'M FROM" POEM EXERCISE

THIS "WHERE I'M FROM" POEM EXERCISE will help you explore your cultural identity and share it with those around you.[1] Don't try too hard to be poetic or cool or compare yourself to other people. Just tell the truth about your childhood background, and then share it with at least one other person. Then listen to their poem. Feel free to fill in the blanks and use the prompts, or go off script if you get inspired—just as long as the listener gets to know you and you get to know yourself.

I am from _____ (traditions that remind you of home),

from _____ (brands—clothing, products, labels commonly used growing up).

I am from _____ (food you ate growing up and holidays you grew up celebrating).

I am from _____ (favorite childhood activities, books you remember most, toys you collected),

from _____ (family member's names or names of people who took care of you).

I am from _____ (plants/gardens that grew inside/outside your home),

from _____ (sounds, touch, scents that remind you of home).

I am from _____ (names of the places your parents are from),

from _____ (names of the places where you've lived).

I am from _____ (phrases you've grown up listening to and superstitions/traditions/oddities your parents/guardians always used).

I am from _____ (activities, adjectives, descriptions that you think best describe your interests growing up).

I am from _____ (faith traditions, faith journey, spiritual discoveries),

from _____ (doubts, struggles with faith).

I am from _____ (phrases or words that remind you of a significant struggle you went through),

from _____ (phrases or words that remind you of great joys in life).

I am from _____ (favorite quotes, mottos you hold dear).

I am _____ (your name).

After you listen to someone share, express your appreciation for sharing their story with you. If you have questions, ask them in humility, not judgment or condescension. Some of the thoughts shared may have been sentimental and were definitely personal. Here are some sentence stems that may help ask good questions:

- I was puzzled when I heard _____. Could you tell me more about that?

- What did you mean when you said _____?

- Could you tell me more about _____?

Please share your poems with us on social media using the hashtag #WhereImFrom.

The following is an example of a "Where I'm From" poem.

"WHERE I'M FROM," JONATHAN WALTON

I am from bacon grease and collard greens,
from hot combs on hot plates and tobacco fields.
I am from the place where hogs outnumber people, and it
smells like chitlins and fried chicken.
I am from the place where pine trees are clear-cut every
fifteen years,
strawberries are small, soft, and sweet, not big, hard,
and green.
I'm from pound cake for birthdays, and work, not rest, over
the holidays,
from the line of Milton and Dorothy Allen.
I am from "Your word is supposed to mean something," and "It
doesn't matter how you feel."
I'm from Sunday morning services where it all looks great, and
master bedrooms with two single beds.
I'm from Fairfax, by way of Brodnax, opposite sides of the
James River,
from Pauline saying to Marvin Walton, "Don't bring that shit
into my house,"
and weekly basketball tournaments with cousins where I only
won once!
from high school football in the fall and soccer in the spring.
I am from pictures on the walls and above the mantle piece,
the "Serenity Prayer" and Psalm 23 at the head of her bed.
I am from 655 Allen Road.
I am Jonathan Paul Walton.

APPENDIX 2

ETHNIC IDENTITY INTERVIEW

1. Download the StoryCorps App. Visit this webpage to get tips, ideas, and best practices:

   - https://storycorps.org/participate/storycorps-app
   - Take some time to listen to some of the most popular interviews on StoryCorps.
   - Now go and do your own!

2. Here is a sample script to start your recording: My name is _____. I am __ years old, and I am here with _____. My hope is to better understand ethnic identity, justice, and reconciliation. Specifically, I want to learn _____ because I don't know _____ and haven't experienced _____. I appreciate _____ taking the time to share his/her story with me.

   - Could you tell me a little about your mom and dad, and where they were from?
   - What were a few of the common sounds and smells in the house where you grew up?
   - What phrases, sayings, or languages stick with you from your childhood?
   - What would a typical meal during the week look like for you? (Example: What was in your school lunch or for dinner on a Tuesday night?)
   - What did you see and hear when you stepped out of your front door?

- Who were some of your favorite people in your neighborhood? Why?

- What are/were some of the experiences that made you feel at home there or unwelcome?

- What are your fears or hesitations about talking about race and racism with white people?

  □ With people of your ethnic identity?

  □ With people of other ethnic backgrounds?

- What advice, warnings, or orders did your parents or grandparents give you about friendships and dating?

- What were the education and career expectations for you?

- How does your family treat its elders?

- What is one thing you wish your white friends understood about you and your background?

- What questions do you wish those from other ethnic backgrounds would ask or not ask?

- What experiences would you invite your friends of different ethnicities to in order to get to know you better?

- What is the most important thing you would like for me and listeners to remember from our time together?

- Thank you so much for sharing your story with me. I really appreciate _____.

The hashtag for this exercise is #12Lies. Please share your interviews with us and others online!

APPENDIX 3

LAMENT, CONFESS, REPENT, RECONCILE

READ 2 CORINTHIANS 5:16-21. The gospel is about restoring shalom—peace in *all* relationships—so humans can create, rule, flourish, and work as he intended. How do we partner with him? How do we become faithful, obedient witnesses?

The following is specific and flexible guidance as you journey with Jesus—not just in the wake of police shootings, sexual assault scandals, or political conflict, but in all places where brokenness reigns and Jesus' kingdom isn't reflected. My hope is that you would lament, confess, repent, and be blessed into the ministry of reconciliation. And I hope you take steps to pray, purchase, partner, and shape policy to see God's personal, relational, and systemic shalom.

1. Acknowledge that these are not isolated incidents. Sexual assault, police brutality, mass shootings, and war are not isolated incidents. Violence between and against people of color (and other vulnerable people) pervades the world. Poverty, inequality, and abortion are not one-off happenings, and the scourge of climate change, greed, self-absorption, sexual violence, and fractured families are part of everyday life, and suffering is constant. Romans 12:15 says to not only rejoice with those who rejoice but to mourn with those who mourn.

2. Ask yourself, Why didn't I engage with this issue/topic/ problem earlier? Ask yourself, *Why didn't I care about this earlier? Why didn't I ask these questions when Trayvon Martin was killed? Or after the shooting at Mother Emanuel Church? Or during the Syrian conflict?*

Note: Don't say "but this is different" and minimize the collective suffering of people of color, women, the poor, those struggling with mental illness, or other vulnerable people (see point 1).

If this is difficult for you, ask yourself the following questions:

- What fears, assumptions, or narratives keep me from entering into the narratives of others about ethnicity, justice, politics, sexual brokenness, and the like? Which of these keep me from entering into my own?

- How have I actively participated in or passively allowed systems of oppression to continue against marginalized people with my words, deeds, or inaction?

3. Please stop talking and listen. Take time to listen to people in pain and those who are immobilized by grief and are wrestling with anger and rage because of the constant suffering and violence in the world.

4. Lament and confess. *Cry.* There is no shame, condemnation, or weakness in weeping. Share with a friend, pastor, or leader why you are angry, sad, and afraid, and allow your emotions to come. Read Psalm 13 or Psalm 88 and rewrite them in your own words.

Confess. It is a violation of God's purposes in this world when we implicitly or explicitly crush the image of God in other people by actively participating in systems and structures that oppress the poor and marginalized or passively allowing these systems to continue. Read Psalm 103 and rewrite it in your own words.

5. Forgiveness and blessing. In Isaiah 6, Isaiah enters into God's holy presence, is convicted of sin, and confesses. Instead of being condemned, he was cleansed and sent out as a witness. Similarly, when we confess our sinfulness before God, he is just and mighty to forgive us, not condemn us.

You may be with people of different ethnicity, background, orientation, or class who you (or your people) are prejudiced against. Ask them to forgive your words, deeds, or silent inaction that has harmed them. Ask them to forgive and bless you as God has forgiven them. A sample forgiveness prayer and blessing are available at the end of the "Lie 7" chapter.

Note: If someone comes to you and asks forgiveness and you grant it, that does not mean you immediately become best friends. Instead, it is a proclamation that you hold no condemnation against them. You are releasing them from the debt they owe you the same way that God has released us from what we owe him in Jesus.

6. *What do repentance and reconciliation look like in practice?* Repentance means to turn, and reconciliation is the restoration of shalom. The LoGOFF Movement's 4Ps are a guide to participate in loving, Spirit-led, Christ-centered reconciliation.

Pray. Alone or with a group, grab your Bible, a journal, and pray! If you don't know how to pray, the Lord's Prayer is a great place to start (see Matthew 6:9-13). You may use the "Teach Us How to Pray" guide available at nycurbanproject.com/resources.

Purchase. Read Psalm 24. In it we learn that "the earth is the LORD's, and all it contains." That means our schedules, finances, the ground we stand on, the air we breathe, and the bodies we have belong to him. Write down the time, talent, and money that you have, and discern how you might offer it back to God on behalf of those affected, because it all belongs to him. The following are some thoughts to get you started:

- Educate yourself on how to break the stigma of those suffering from depression, PTSD, and other forms of mental illness. How much time do you want to allocate for this work?

- Spend time in a community much different from yours to learn at the feet of those who are a different race, class, gender, or status. How much time do you want to set aside for this activity?

- Educate yourself on the realities of gun violence in America. How much time do you want to set aside for this activity?

- Give $50 a month to a ministry, fund, or advocacy organization serving those killed by violence, suffering under oppression, or escaping from human trafficking.

- Volunteer your talents in organizing, accounting, communication, or art to take an internship for a year, or join a local group pursuing the values you hear from Scripture, prayer, and biblical teaching.

- Look at the time, talent, and treasure before you (not just the *extra* you *think* you have) and offer it back to God because he gave it to you!

Partner. With the time, talent, and treasure you brought to God, look for partners to help you leverage them for the poor, marginalized, and oppressed—and then follow through! Email, call, and follow up. God's work, particularly for justice, is hard, long-term, and full of triumphs and tragedies. Keep in mind the truth that success is not in the progress you make but in your obedience to the God who loves us.

Policy making. After prayer, building relationships, and investing our time, talents, and resources for God's glory, we may be adequately informed and formed to protest, petition, and participate in political advocacy and activism necessary for systemic transformation.[1]

For a larger, more detailed framework, please visit nycurbanproject .com/resources. If you have questions or concerns about this document or resources, please email jonathan.walton@intervarsity.org.

NOTES

INTRODUCTION: THE LIES THAT BIND

[1] This paragraph, along with other sentences and paragraphs sprinkled throughout the manuscript, have been taken from the author's blog posts (nycurbanproject.com/blog) on September 22, 2016; October 3, 2016; November 9, 2016; March 26, 2017; and April 29, 2017; and at InterVarsity's NYC Urban Project, www.nycurbanproject.com/blog/?author=53d47122e4 b0498d331c77ad.

[2] Christianna Silva, "Why Are so Many Native Americans Killed by Police?," *Newsweek*, November 11, 2017, www.newsweek.com/more-native-americans -are-being-killed-police-including-14-year-old-who-might-708728; and Maria Perez, "It's Not Just Black and White People: Police Shootings Are Killing Latinos," *Newsweek*, September 23, 2017, www.newsweek.com/latinos-police -shootings-oklahoma-city-669854.

[3] Jon Swaine, Oliver Laughland, Jamiles Lartey, and Ciara McCarthy, "Young Black Men Killed by US Police at Highest Rate in Year of 1,134 Deaths," *Guardian*, December 31, 2015, www.theguardian.com/us-news/2015 /dec/31/the-counted-police-killings-2015-young-black-men.

[4] Tom McCarthy, Jon Swaine, and Oliver Laughland, "FBI to Launch New System to Count People Killed by Police Officers," *Guardian*, December 8, 2015, www.theguardian.com/us-news/2015/dec/09/fbi-launch-new-system -count-people-killed-police-officers-the-counted; Todd C. Frankel, "Why the CDC Still Isn't Researching Gun Violence, Despite the Ban Being Lifted Two Years Ago," *Washington Post*, January 14, 2015, www.washingtonpost.com /news/storyline/wp/2015/01/14/why-the-cdc-still-isnt-researching-gun -violence-despite-the-ban-being-lifted-two-years-ago/?utm_term =.cd53143ea143.

[5] Louis Jacobson, "Bill Bennett Understates His Point on Black Murder Victims," *Politifact*, July 28, 2009, www.politifact.com/truth-o-meter /statements /2009/jul/28/bill-bennett/black-men-are-4-percent-americans -35-percent-murde/.

[6] Katherine Stewart, "Eighty-One Percent of White Evangelicals Voted for Donald Trump. Why?," *Nation*, November 17, 2016, www.thenation.com /article/eighty-one-percent-of-white-evangelicals-voted-for-donald

-trump-why; Jon Huang, Samuel Jacoby, Michael Strickland, and K. K. Rebecca Lai, "Election 2016: Exit Polls," *New York Times*, November 8, 2016, www.nytimes.com/interactive/2016/11/08/us/politics/election -exit-polls.html.

[7]White = manmade racial-gender-class-culture-based hierarchy. American = national identity defined by citizenship and the level of adoption and mastery of whiteness. Folk religion = common set of popular beliefs and practices under the umbrella of a religion but is outside of the religion's official doctrines and practices.

[8]"Who Got the Right to Vote When?," *Al Jazeera*, accessed May 15, 2018, https://interactive.aljazeera.com/aje/2016/us-elections-2016-who-can-vote /index.html.

[9]Sarah Pruitt, "5 Things You May Not Know About Lincoln, Slavery and Emancipation," History.com, September 21, 2012, www.history.com/news /5-things-you-may-not-know-about-lincoln-slavery-and-emancipation.

[10]"Gentlemen's Agreement," *Densho Encyclopedia*, accessed May 15, 2018, http://encyclopedia.densho.org/Gentlemen's%20Agreement.

[11]"History of Voting Rights," MassVote, accessed May 15, 2018, http:// massvote.org.

[12]"History of Voting Rights."

[13]Adam Cohen, "The Supreme Court Ruling That Led to 70,000 Forced Sterilizations," *Fresh Air*, NPR, interview by David Bianculli, March 7, 2016, www.npr.org/2017/03/24/521360544/the-supreme-court-ruling-that-led -to-70-000-forced-sterilizations.

[14]Francisco Balderrama, "America's Forgotten History of Mexican-American 'Repatriation,'" *Fresh Air*, NPR, interview by Terry Gross, September 10, 2015, www.npr.org/2015/09/10/439114563/americas-forgotten-history -of-mexican-american-repatriation.

[15]Sushma Subramanian, "Worse Than Tuskegee," Slate.com, February 26, 2017, http://www.slate.com/articles/health_and_science/cover_story/2017 /02/guatemala_syphilis_experiments_worse_than_tuskegee.html.

[16]Peter Chapman, *Bananas: How the United Fruit Company Shaped the World* (New York: Canongate Books, 2009).

[17]"Voting Rights in the United States: Prisoners," Wikipedia, accessed May 15, 2018, https://en.wikipedia.org/wiki/Voting_rights_in_the_United _States#Prisoners.

[18]*Malcom X*, directed by Spike Lee (Los Angeles: Warner Bros., 1992).

LIE 1. WE ARE A CHRISTIAN NATION

[1]Marius Artemis, "Desiring God's John Piper Says He Believes That Women Shouldn't Teach in Seminaries," *Christian Daily*, February 18, 2018, www .christiandaily.com/article/desiring-gods-john-piper-says-he-believes-that -women-shouldnt-teach-in-seminaries/61920.htm.

[2]Jeremy Weber, "80% of Churchgoers Don't Read Bible Daily, LifeWay Survey Suggests," *Christianity Today*, September 7, 2012, www.christianitytoday.com /news/2012/september/80-of-churchgoers-dont-read-bible-daily-lifeway -survey.html; "New Research on the State of Discipleship," Barna, December 1, 2015, www.barna.com/research/new-research-on-the-state-of-discipleship.

[3]"The Goal," United Northern and Southern Knights of the Ku Klux Klan, July 13, 2018, www.unskkkk.com.

[4]"Protestant Ethic," *English Oxford Living Dictionaries*, accessed May 2, 2018, https://en.oxforddictionaries.com/definition/us/Protestant_ethic.

[5]George W. Bush, "Bush Shopping Quote," C-SPAN, September 28, 2015, www.c-span.org/video/?c4552776/bush-shopping-quote.

[6]Barack Obama, "Obama's Inaugural Speech," CNN, January 20, 2009, www .cnn.com/2009/POLITICS/01/20/obama.politics.

[7]Michael Fisher, "The Ku Klux Klan," Touchstone, accessed May 21, 2018, http://home.wlu.edu/~lubint/touchstone/KKK-Fisher.htm.

[8]Victor Lebow, quoted in Andrew Martin, "Consume, Consume, Consume with the False Promise of Happiness," *Collective Evolution*, July 17, 2014, www.collective-evolution.com/2014/07/17/consume-consume-consume -with-the-false-promise-of-happiness.

[9]Martin Luther King Jr., "Sermon at Temple Israel of Hollywood," *American Rhetoric*, February 26, 1965, www.americanrhetoric.com/speeches /mlktempleisraelhollywood.htm.

[10]Matt Lewis, "Obama Loves Martin Luther King's Great Quote—But He Uses It Incorrectly," *Daily Beast*, January 16, 2017, www.thedailybeast.com /obama-loves-martin-luther-kings-great-quotebut-he-uses-it-incorrectly.

[11]Julian the Apostate, quoted in Michael Craven, "The Christian Conquest of Pagan Rome," Crosswalk.com, November 8, 2010, www.crosswalk.com/blogs /michael-craven/the-christian-conquest-of-pagan-rome-11640691.html.

LIE 2. WE ALL ARE IMMIGRANTS

[1]Ben Carson, quoted in Tracy Jan and Jose A. DelReal, "Carson Compares Slaves to Immigrants Coming to 'a Land of Dreams and Opportunity,'" *Washington*

Post, March 6, 2017, www.washingtonpost.com/news/wonk/wp/2017/03/06
/carson-compares-slaves-to-immigrants-coming-to-a-land-of-dreams-and
-opportunity.

[2]Tony Perkins, quoted in Edward-Isaac Dovere, "Tony Perkins: Trump Gets
'a Mulligan' on Life, Stormy Daniels," *Politico*, January 23, 2018, www.politico
.com/magazine/story/2018/01/23/tony-perkins-evangelicals-donald
-trump-stormy-daniels-216498.

[3]Owen Lindauer, "About the Phoenix Indian School," Modern American
Poetry, accessed May 22, 2018, www.english.illinois.edu/maps/poets/a_f
/erdrich/boarding/phoenix.htm.

[4]Jonathan Lipnick, "What Did the Israelite Slaves Build in Egypt?," Israel Institute of Biblical Studies, October 9, 2016, https://blog.israelbiblicalstudies
.com/holy-land-studies/1483-2.

LIE 3. WE ARE A MELTING POT

[1]"Loving v. Virginia," Oyez.org, accessed May 23, 2018, www.oyez.org
/cases/1966/395.

[2]Emma Brown, "The Overwhelming Whiteness of U.S. Private Schools, in Six
Maps and Charts," *Washington Post*, March 29, 2016, www.washingtonpost
.com/news/education/wp/2016/03/29/the-overwhelming-whiteness-of-u
-s-private-schools-in-six-maps-and-charts/?utm_term=.cc59cfd9ac1c.

[3]Michael Barbaro, "Listen to 'The Daily': Linda Brown's Landmark Case," *New
York Times*, March 30, 2018, www.nytimes.com/2018/03/30/podcasts/the
-daily/linda-brown-board-of-education.html.

[4]"'Kill the Indian, and Save the Man': Capt. Richard H. Pratt on the Education
of Native Americans," History Matters, accessed May 23, 2018, http://his-
torymatters.gmu.edu/d/4929.

[5]Israel Zangwill, *The Melting Pot* in Gary Gerstle, *American Crucible: Race and
Nation in the Twentieth Century* (Princeton, NJ: Princeton University Press,
2001), 51.

[6]Luis Bush, "The Meaning of Ethne in Matthew 28:18," *Mission Frontiers*,
September 1, 2013, www.missionfrontiers.org/issue/article/the-meaning
-of-ethne-in-matthew-2819.

LIE 4. ALL MEN ARE CREATED EQUAL

[1]Editorial Projects in Education Research Center, "Tracking," *Education Week*,
August 4, 2004, www.edweek.org/ew/issues/tracking/index.html.

[2]See The Governor's School of Southside Virginia, http://gssv.southside.edu; and "The Named Scholars," Berick Center for Student Advising, Columbia College, www.cc-seas.columbia.edu/scholars/named.

[3]Pat Robertson, quoted in "Pat Robertson Says Haiti Paying for 'Pact to the Devil,'" CNN, January 13, 2010, www.cnn.com/2010/US/01/13/haiti.pat .robertson/index.html.

[4]James Doubek, "Oklahoma Police Fatally Shoot Deaf Man Despite Yells of 'He Can't Hear,'" NPR, September 21, 2017, www.npr.org/sections/thetwo way/2017/09/21/552527929/oklahoma-city-police-fatally-shoot -deaf-man-despite-yells-of-he-cant-hear-you.

[5]"Fatal Force," *Washington Post*, accessed May 25, 2018, www.washingtonpost .com/graphics/national/police-shootings-2017.

[6]Kimberly Yam, "Single Mom Graduates from College to Set 'First Example' for Son," *HuffPost*, May 17, 2016, www.huffingtonpost.com/entry/single -moms-tearful-photo-with-son-after-graduation-shows-how-grateful-she -is-for-him_us_573b3190e4b077d4d6f40fdb.

[7]Bill Laitner, "Heart and Sole: Detroiter Walks 21 Miles in Work Commute," *Detroit Free Press*, January 31, 2015, www.freep.com/story/news/local /michigan/oakland/2015/01/31/detroit-commuting-troy-rochester-hills -smart-ddot-ubs-banker-woodward-buses-transit/22660785.

[8]Liam Stack, "Video Released in Terence Crutcher's Killing by Tulsa Police," *New York Times*, September 19, 2016, www.nytimes.com/2016/09/20/us /video-released-in-terence-crutchers-killing-by-tulsa-police.html.

[9]Franklin Graham, "Listen up, whites, blacks, Latinos, and everybody else," Facebook, September 25, 2016, www.facebook.com/FranklinGraham /posts/1260074277382084.

[10]Dara Maclean and Paul Mabury, "Blameless," *Wanted*, Fervent Records, 2013. Used with permission.

[11]Jonathan Walton, "Franklin Graham Doesn't See Me, but Jesus Does," New York City Urban Project, October 3, 2016, www.nycurbanproject.com /blog/3/10/2016/franklin-graham-doesnt-see-me-but-jesus-does#.

[12]See James H. Cone, *The Cross and the Lynching Tree* (Maryknoll, NY: Orbis Books, 2011); and "Freedom Struggle," National Museum of American History, accessed May 30, 2018, http://americanhistory.si.edu/brown /history/6-legacy/freedom-struggle-2.html.

[13]James Madison, quoted in *Secret Proceedings of the Constitutional Debates of the Convention Assembled at Philadelphia, in the Year 1787* (Louisville,

KY: Alston Mygatt, 1844), 182, https://archive.org/stream/secretproceed in00convgoog#page/n8/mode/2up/search/opulent.

[14]"Shooting of Philando Castile," Wikipedia, accessed May 30, 2018, https:// en.wikipedia.org/wiki/Shooting_of_Philando_Castile; and "Shooting of Alton Sterling," Wikipedia, accessed May 30, 2018, https://en.wikipedia .org/wiki/Shooting_of_Alton_Sterling.

[15]William Arkin, Tracy Connor, and Jim Miklaszewski, "Dallas Shooter Micah Johnson Was Army Veteran and 'Loner,'" NBC News, July 8, 2016, www .nbcnews.com/storyline/dallas-police-ambush/dallas-shooter-micah -xavier-johnson-was-army-veteran-n606101; "The Counted," *Guardian*, ac- cessed July 16, 2018, www.theguardian.com/us-news/ng-interactive /2015/jun/01/the-counted-police-killings-us-database#.

[16]Wes Lowery, "Graphic Video Shows Daniel Shaver Sobbing and Begging Officer for His Life Before 2016 Shooting," *Washington Post*, December 8, 2017, www.washingtonpost.com/news/post-nation/wp/2017/12/08 /graphic-video-shows-daniel-shaver-sobbing-and-begging-officer-for-his -life-before-2016-shooting; and Eli Rosenberg and Herman Wong, "A Police Officer Fatally Shot a Man While Responding to an Emergency Call Now Called a 'Swatting' Prank," *Washington Post*, December 30, 2017, www.washingtonpost.com/news/post-nation/wp/2017/12/29/a-police -officer-fatally-shot-a-man-while-responding-to-an-emergency-call -now-called-a-swatting-prank/?utm.

[17]Ricardo A. Sunga III, "UN Expert Group Condemns Recent Killings," United Nations Human Rights, July 8, 2016, www.ohchr.org/EN/NewsEvents /Pages/DisplayNews.aspx?NewsID=20248&LangID=E.

LIE 5. WE ARE A GREAT DEMOCRACY

[1]Alan Rappeport, "'What Is 'Aleppo?' Gary Johnson Asks, in an Interview Stumble," *New York Times*, September 8, 2016, www.nytimes .com/2016/09/09/us/politics/gary-johnson-aleppo.html.

[2]Aleppo is a Syrian city devastated by the civil war and atrocities of the Bashar al-Assad regime. The US government authorized military force in Syria in 2013. See "United States Involvement in Syria, 2009-2017," BallotPedia, accessed June 5, 2018, https://ballotpedia.org/United_States _involvement_in_Syria,_2009-2017.

[3]James Madison, quoted in Steve Straub, "Federalist 10, Democracies Have Ever Been Spectacles of Turbulence and Contention," *Federalist Papers*, July

31, 2012, https://thefederalistpapers.org/federalist-papers/federalist-10-democracies-have-ever-been-spectacles-of-turbulence-and-contention.

[4]Alexander Hamilton, quoted in Steve Straub, "Alexander Hamilton, Real Liberty Is Neither Found in Despotism or the Extremes of Democracy, but in Moderate Governments," *Federalist Papers*, July 12, 2012, https://thefederalistpapers.org/founders/hamilton/alexander-hamilton-real-liberty-is-neither-found-in-despotism-or-the-extremes-of-democracy-but-in-moderate-governments.

[5]John Adams, *The Letters of John and Abigail Adams*, Goodreads, accessed June 5, 2018, www.goodreads.com/quotes/49810-i-do-not-say-that-democracy-has-been-more-pernicious.

[6]*The 21st-Century Voter: Who Votes, How They Vote, and Why They Vote*, eds. Guido H. Stempel III and Thomas K. Hargrove (Santa Barbara, CA: ABC-CLIO, LLC, 2016), 446.

[7]"Who Got the Right to Vote When?," *Al Jazeera*, accessed May 15, 2018, https://interactive.aljazeera.com/aje/2016/us-elections-2016-who-can-vote/index.html.

[8]"Jim Crow Laws," PBS, accessed June 5, 2018, www.pbs.org/wgbh/americanexperience/features/freedom-riders-jim-crow-laws.

[9]"Dec. 25, 1951: Bombing of the Moore Family Home in Florida," Zinn Education Project, accessed June 5, 2018, https://zinnedproject.org/2014/12/moore-home-bombed.

[10]See Vann R. Newkirk, "How Voter ID Laws Discriminate," *Atlantic*, February 18, 2017, www.theatlantic.com/politics/archive/2017/02/how-voter-id-laws-discriminate-study/517218; and Ben Schreckinger, "White Nationalists Plot Election Day Show of Force," Politico, November 2, 2016, www.politico.com/story/2016/11/suppress-black-vote-trump-campaign-230616.

[11]Michael Wines and Alan Blinder, "Federal Appeals Court Strikes Down North Carolina Voter ID Requirement," *New York Times*, July 29, 2016, www.nytimes.com/2016/07/30/us/federal-appeals-court-strikes-down-north-carolina-voter-id-provision.html.

[12]Marc Caputo, "Gov. Rick Scott Looks Ready to Fight DOJ over Voter Purge," *Miami Herald*, June 5, 2012, www.miamiherald.com/news/politics-government/article1940392.html.

[13]Christopher Ingraham, "This Is the Best Explanation of Gerrymandering You Will Ever See," *Washington Post*, March 1, 2010, www.washingtonpost.com/news/wonk/wp/2015/03/01/this-is-the-best-explanation-of-gerrymandering-you-will-ever-see/?utm_term=.145fc100fab1.

[14]Emily Barasch, "The Twisted History of Gerrymandering in American Politics," *Atlantic*, September 19, 2012, www.theatlantic.com/politics/archive/2012/09/the-twisted-history-of-gerrymandering-in-american-politics/262369/#slide3.

[15]David Lewis, quoted in John Oliver, "Gerrymandering," *Last Week Tonight with John Oliver*, April 9, 2010, www.youtube.com/watch?v=A-4dIImaodQ&t=537s.

[16]Jeremy Mayer, quoted in Oliver, "Gerrymandering."

[17]Oliver, "Gerrymandering."

[18]"Hakeem Jeffries," Wikipedia, accessed June 5, 2018, https://en.wikipedia.org/wiki/Hakeem_Jeffries.

[19]"Lobbying," WikiVisually, accessed June 6, 2018, https://wikivisually.com/wiki/Lobbying.

[20]"Citizens United v. FEC," Bill of Rights Institute, February 14, 2017, www.youtube.com/watch?v=4J5Zx5YotBU.

[21]Tom Murse, "How Much Did the Obama Campaign Cost?," ThoughtCo, April 23, 2017, www.thoughtco.com/cost-of-the-obama-campaign-3367606.

[22]Anu Narayanswamy, Darla Cameron, and Matera Gold, "Money Raised as of Dec. 31," *Washington Post*, February 1, 2017, www.washingtonpost.com/graphics/politics/2016-election/campaign-finance.

[23]Kimberly Kindy, "Spending on Lobbying Approached $1 Billion in First Quarter, Highest," *Washington Post*, April 25, 2017, www.washingtonpost.com/national/spending-on-lobbying-approached-1-billion-in-first-quarter-highest-in-5-years/2017/04/25/0ab469f6-2910-11e7-be51-b3fc6ff7faee_story.html.

[24]KSDK Staff, "Trump, Pence Allies Rake in Millions as New Washington Lobbyists," KSDK.com, April 23, 2017, www.ksdk.com/article/news/politics/national-politics/trump-pence-allies-rake-in-millions-as-new-washington-lobbyists/433572427.

[25]Drew DeSilver, "Turnout Was High in the 2016 Primary Season, but Just Short of 2008 Record," Pew Research Center, June 10, 2016, www.pewresearch.org/fact-tank/2016/06/10/turnout-was-high-in-the-2016-primary-season-but-just-short-of-2008-record; and Jens Manuel Krogstad and Mark Hugo Lopez, "Black Voter Turnout Fell in 2016, even as a Record Number of Americans Cast Ballots," Pew Research Center, May 12, 2017, www.pewresearch.org/fact-tank/2017/05/12/black-voter-turnout-fell-in-2016-even-as-a-record-number-of-americans-cast-ballots.

[26]Kristen Hubby, "How Many Americans Actually Vote," Daily Dot, December 19, 2016, www.dailydot.com/layer8/voter-turnout-2016.

[27]"1787: Constitutional Convention Begins," *History*, accessed June 5, 2017, www.history.com/this-day-in-history/constitutional-convention-begins; and "44th ALEC Annual Meeting—Denver, Co," ALEC, July 19-21, 2017, www.alec.org/meeting/2017-annual-meeting-denver-co.

[28]Lawrence Mishel and Alyssa Davis, "Top CEOs Make 300 Times More Than Typical Workers," Economic Policy Institute, June 21, 2015, www.epi.org /publication/top-ceos-make-300-times-more-than-workers-pay-growth -surpasses-market-gains-and-the-rest-of-the-0-1-percent; Tom Kertscher, "Bernie Sanders, in Madison, Claims Top 0.1% of Americans Have Almost as Much Wealth as Bottom 90%," Politifact, July 29, 2015, www.politifact .com/wisconsin/statements/2015/jul/29/bernie-s/bernie-sanders -madison-claims-top-01-americans-hav; and Brad Plumer, "Why More Than 80 Million Americans Won't Vote on Election Day," Vox.com, November 8, 2016, www.vox.com/policy-and-politics/2016/11/7/13536198/election -day-americans-vote.

LIE 6. THE AMERICAN DREAM IS ALIVE AND WELL

[1]Kif Leswing, "Apple Just Broke Its Own Record as the Most Valuable Publicly Traded Company of All Time," *Business Insider*, May 8, 2017, www.business insider.com/apple-becomes-the-most-valuable-publicly-traded-company -of-all-time-2017-5.

[2]Donald Trump, quoted in Michelle Rotuno-Johnson, "Trump in 2005: 'When You Are a Star . . . You Can Do Anything' to Women," NBC4.com, October 7, 2016, www.nbc4i.com/news/u-s-world/trump-in-2005-when -youre-a-star-you-can-do-anything-to-women/1065147642.

[3]Jodi Kantor and Megan Twohey, "Harvey Weinstein Paid Off Sexual Ha- rassment Accusers for Decades," *New York Times*, October 5, 2017, www .nytimes.com/2017/10/05/us/harvey-weinstein-harassment-allegations .html; and Kim Bellware, "Here Are the Women Publicly Accusing Roger Ailes of Sexual Harassment," *HuffPost*, August 12, 2016, www.huffingtonpost .com/entry/roger-ailes-accusers-list_us_57a9fa19e4b06e52746db865.

LIE 7. WE ARE THE MOST PROSPEROUS NATION IN THE WORLD

[1]Chris Matthews, "Fortune 5: The Most Powerful Economic Empires of

All Time," October 5, 2014, http://fortune.com/2014/10/05/most
-powerful-economic-empires-of-all-time.

[2] Dave Tilford, quoted in "Use It and Lose It: The Outsize Effect of U.S. Consumption on the Environment," *Scientific American*, accessed June 7, 2018, www.scientificamerican.com/article/american-consumption-habits.

[3] Scarlet, "Statistics That Will Make You Want to Recycle Your Cell Phone," SC Johnson, February 15, 2012, www.scjohnson.com/en/green-choices /Reduce-and-Recycle/Articles/Article-Details.aspx?date=12-02 -15&title=Statistics-That-Will-Make-You-Want-To-Recycle-Your-Cell -Phone; Elizabeth Kirk, "Recycling with Sole," Waste 360, April 1, 2010, www.waste360.com/Recycling_And_Processing/shoe-recycling-201004; and Janine Satioquia-Tan, "Americans Eat HOW MUCH Chocolate?," CNBC, July 23, 2015, www.cnbc.com/2015/07/23/americans-eat-how-much -chocolate.html.

[4] Tim Keller, "We Can't See Our Own Greed," *Preaching Today*, March 2011, www.preachingtoday.com/illustrations/2011/march/6030711.html.

[5] "Confession of Sin," Presbyterian Mission Agency: Resources on Cultural Diversity and Racism.

LIE 8. WE ARE THE MOST GENEROUS PEOPLE IN THE WORLD

[1] Lee C. Bollinger, "John Kluge, CC'37, Pledges $400 Million for Financial Aid— Cloned," Columbia University, April 11, 2007, https://president.columbia .edu/news/john-kluge-cc37-pledges-400-million-financial-aid-cloned.

[2] Jonathan Walton, "Invisible Children." This poem first appeared in my book *Legal: The First 21 Years* (Mustang, OK: Tate Publishing, 2008).

[3] Alex Daniels and Anu Narayanswamy, "The Income-Inequality Divide Hits Generosity," *The Chronicle of Philanthropy*, October 5, 2014, www .philanthropy.com/article/The-Income-Inequality-Divide/15255.

[4] James McBride, "How Does the U.S. Spend Its Foreign Aid?," Council of Foreign Relations, April 11, 2017, www.cfr.org/backgrounder/how-does-us -spend-its-foreign-aid.

[5] McBride, "How Does the U.S. Spend Its Foreign Aid?"

[6] "Policy Basics: Where Do Our Federal Tax Dollars Go?," Center on Budget and Policy Priorities, October 4, 2017, www.cbpp.org/research/federal -budget/policy-basics-where-do-our-federal-tax-dollars-go; and Louis Jacobson, "Pie Chart of 'Federal Spending' Circulating on the Internet Is Misleading," August 17, 2015, www.politifact.com/truth-o-meter

/statements/2015/aug/17/facebook-posts/pie-chart-federal-spending -circulating-internet-mi.

[7]Daniel B. Kline, "Where Do Your Tax Dollars Actually Go?," *Motley Fool*, April 6, 2017, www.fool.com/taxes/2017/04/06/where-do-your-tax-dollars -actually-go.aspx; and "Giving USA: 2015 Was America's Most-Generous Year Ever," Giving USA, June 13, 2016, https://givingusa.org/giving-usa-2016.

[8]"The Truth About Christians Tithing in the U.S.," *Share Faith*, accessed June 8, 2018, www.sharefaith.com/blog/2015/12/facts-christians-tithing; and "Statistics on U.S. Generosity," Philanthropy Roundtable, accessed June 8, 2018, www.philanthropyroundtable.org/almanac/statistics/u.s.-generosity.

[9]Bruce Waltke, quoted in Timothy Keller, *Generous Justice* (New York: Penguin, 2012), 87.

[10]Dionysius, quote in Jeremiah, "The Everyday Martyrdom," *Orthodox Road* (blog), accessed June 8, 2018, www.orthodoxroad.com/the-everyday -martyrdom/#more-1685.

[11]Church Communities Foundation, "Eberhard Arnold's Life and Work," Erberhardarnold.com, accessed September 7, 2018, www.eberhardarnold .com/biography.html.

[12]Emmy Arnold, "A Joyful Pilgrimage," Bruderhof.com, accessed June 8, 2018, www.bruderhof.com/en/our-faith/resources/publications-about-the -bruderhof/a-joyful-pilgrimage.

LIE 9. AMERICA IS THE LAND OF THE FREE

[1]Donald H. Rumsfeld, "The Price of Freedom in Iraq," *New York Times*, March 19, 2004, www.nytimes.com/2004/03/19/opinion/the-price-of-freedom -in-iraq.html; "Operation Iraqi Freedom and Operation New Dawn Fast Facts," CNN Library, March 8, 2018, www.cnn.com/2013/10/30/world/meast /operation-iraqi-freedom-and-operation-new-dawn-fast-facts/index.html; Julian Borger, "There Were No Weapons of Mass Destruction in Iraq," *Guardian*, October 7, 2004, www.theguardian.com/world/2004/oct/07/usa .iraq1; and James Meikle, "George Bush Thought 9/11 Plane Shot Down on His Orders," *Guardian*, October 29, 2010, www.theguardian.com /world/2010/oct/29/george-bush-thought-9-11-plane-shot-down.

[2]Lauren Carroll, "Trump: Eisenhower Deported 1.5 Million Immigrants," Politifact, November 11, 2015, www.politifact.com/truth-o-meter/state ments/2015/nov/11/donald-trump/trump-eisenhower-deported-15-million -immigrants; and "Japanese Internment Camps," *History*, accessed June 18, 2018, www.history.com/topics/world-war-ii/japanese-american-relocation.

3"The Rise of ISIS," *Frontline*, October 28, 2014, www.pbs.org/wgbh/frontline /film/rise-of-isis.

4Rumsfeld, "The Price of Freedom in Iraq."

5Rumsfeld, "The Price of Freedom in Iraq."

6A. J. Willingham, "Study Finds 1 in 8 Americans Struggles with Alcohol Abuse," CNN, August 11, 2017, www.cnn.com/2017/08/10/health/drinking -alcoholism-study-trnd/index.html; "Get the Facts and Figures," National Domestic Violence Hotline, accessed June 18, 2018, www.thehotline.org /resources/statistics; Leo Shane III and Patricia Kime, "New VA Study Finds 20 Veterans Commit Suicide Each Day," *Military Times*, July 7, 2016, www .militarytimes.com/veterans/2016/07/07/new-va-study-finds-20-veterans -commit-suicide-each-day; and "Nearly Half of American Children Living Near Poverty Line," Columbia University, March 3, 2016, www.mailman .columbia.edu/public-health-now/news/nearly-half-american-children -living-near-poverty-line.

LIE 10. AMERICA IS THE HOME OF THE BRAVE

1*Taken*, directed by Pierre Morel (Paris: EuropaCorp, 2008).

2"The New Abolitionists: Who Are They?," New York's New Abolitionists, ac-cessed June 19, 2018, www.newyorksnewabolitionists.com.

3John Winthrop, quoted in "Massachusetts Bay—'The City upon a Hill,'" U.S. History, accessed June 19, 2018, www.ushistory.org/us/3c.asp.

4"About," Moton Museum, accessed June 19, 2018, www.motonmuseum.org /about.

5Sarah Flower Adams, "Nearer, My God, to Thee," 1841.

6Stephen J. Dubner, "Who Serves in the Military Today?," Freakonomics, September 22, 2008, http://freakonomics.com/2008/09/22/who-serves -in-the-military-today; and Bill Bishop, "Soldiers' Death Rate Reveals 'Two Americas,'" *Daily Yonder*, October 4, 2016, www.dailyyonder.com/soldiers-death-rate-reveals-two-americas/2016/10/04/15621.

7Dubner, "Who Serves in the Military Today?"

LIE 11. AMERICA IS THE GREATEST COUNTRY ON EARTH

1Dinesh D'Souza, "10 Great Things," *National Review*, July 2, 2003, www .nationalreview.com/2003/07/10-great-things-dinesh-dsouza.

2Dinesh D'Souza, quoted in David Weigel, "Newt Is Nuts!," *Slate*, September

13, 2010, www.slate.com/articles/news_and_politics/politics/2010/09
/newt_is_nuts.html.

[3]"Kids from USA Rank #1 in Confidence," *YouTube*, January 5, 2017, www
.youtube.com/watch?v=ɛtkimTc_Pi4.

[4]George Washington, "Transcript of President George Washington's First
Inaugural Speech (1789)," OurDocuments.gov, accessed June 19, 2018,
www.ourdocuments.gov/doc.php?flash=true&doc=11&page=transcript.

[5]"George Washington Letter Describes Killing of Natives as 'Villainy,'" *Indian
Country Today*, June 6, 2013, https://indiancountrymedianetwork.com
/history/events/george-washington-letter-describes-killing-of-natives-as
-villainy; and Tyler Rogoway, "The Revolutionary War: By the Numbers,"
Jalopnik.com, July 4, 2014, https://foxtrotalpha.jalopnik.com/the
-revolutionary-war-by-the-numbers-1600199390.

[6]Mark Krieg, Tim Spirk, La-Kita Gilmore, and Dave Hess, "The Year of Ju-
bilee," Christ Community Church, January 3, 2016, www.christcc.org
/audio/sermons/2016-01-03_team.pdf.

[7]Salma Hayek, "Harvey Is My Monster Too," *New York Times*, December 13,
2017, www.nytimes.com/interactive/2017/12/13/opinion/contributors
/salma-hayek-harvey-weinstein.html.

LIE 12. WE ARE ONE NATION

[1]"Racial Disparity," Sentencing Project, accessed June 20, 3018, www
.sentencingproject.org/issues/racial-disparity; Nicole Hannah Jones, "The
Resegregation of Jefferson County," *New York Times*, September 6, 2017,
www.nytimes.com/2017/09/06/magazine/the-resegregation-of-jefferson
-county.html; and "Voter Suppression Laws: What's New Since the 2012
Presidential Election," ACLU, accessed June 20, 2018, www.aclu.org/map
/voter-suppression-laws-whats-new-2012-presidential-election.

[2]Jennifer Calfas, "Trump Supporter Apologizes to Protester for Punching
Him," *The Hill*, December 14, 2016, http://thehill.com/blogs/blog
-briefing-room/news/310484-trump-supporter-who-sucker-punched
-protester-apologizes; and Bryan Armen Graham, "Donald Trump Blasts
NFL Anthem Protesters: 'Get That Son of a Bitch off the Field,'" *Guardian*,
September 23, 2017, www.theguardian.com/sport/2017/sep/22/donald
-trump-nfl-national-anthem-protests.

[3]"Trump Supporter Who Punched Protester: Next Time, We Might Have to Kill
Him," *YouTube*, March 10, 2016, www.youtube.com/watch?v=DzU3FLZgIhc.

4Graham, "Donald Trump Blasts NFL Anthem Protesters."

5"Fatal Force," *Washington Post*, accessed July 16, 2018, www.washingtonpost
.com/graphics/national/police-shootings-2017.

6Matthew Hutson, "Why Liberals Aren't as Tolerant as They Think," *Politico*,
May 9, 2017, www.politico.com/magazine/story/2017/05/09/why-liberals
-arent-as-tolerant-as-they-think-215114.

7Wes Enzinna, "This Is War and We Intend to Win," *Mother Jones*, May-June
2017, www.motherjones.com/politics/2017/04/anti-racist-antifa-tinley
-park-five/#. Regarding the ARA, see "Columbus, Ohio, Holocaust Memorial
Reportback & Partial d0x," Anti-Racist Actions, accessed June 20, 2017,
https://antiracistaction.org. see www.youtube.com/watch?v=DzU3FLZgIhc.

8Wes Enzinna, "Left Hook: A Brief History of Nazi Punching in America,"
Mother Jones, May-June 2017, www.motherjones.com/politics/2017/04
/timeline-anti-fascists-nazi-punching/.

9"The Pledge of Allegiance," USHistory.org, accessed June 20, 3018, www
.ushistory.org/documents/pledge.htm.

10"Barak Obama's Feb. 5 Speech," *New York Times*, February 5, 2008, www
.nytimes.com/2008/02/05/us/politics/05text-obama.html.

11Leo Tolstoy, *Anna Karenina*, trans. Joel Carmichael (New York: Random
House Bantam Classic, 1981), 1.

12Frances Allitsen, "The Lord Is My Light," 1897.

APPENDIX 1

1This exercise is taken from "Week 46: Community Values Part 3—
Hospitality," Year of Biblical Literacy, accessed June 20, 2018, http://bible
.realitysf.com/small-group-material/week-46. Adapted from the poem
"Where I'm From" by George Ella Lyon; see the I Am From Project website,
https://iamfromproject.com.

APPENDIX 3

1This information first appeared in Jonathan Walton, "What We Can Do
After Praying for Victims of Another Mass Shooting," *HuffPost*, October 2,
2016, www.huffingtonpost.com/jonathan-walton/praying-for-victims
_b_8233938.html.

ABOUT THE AUTHOR

Jonathan Walton is the director of experiential discipleship for InterVarsity NY/NJ and leads New York City Urban Project (NYCUP). He founded the LoGOFF Movement and is cofounder of Making Stewards. He writes regularly for Medium .com and is the author of three books of poetry and short stories. He is a member of New Life Fellowship and lives with his wife, daughter, and dog in New York City.